# METHODS
## A JOURNAL OF ACTING PEDAGOGY

Volume 2, 2016
Pace University Press

Copyright © 2016
Pace University Press
41 Park Row, 15th Floor
New York, NY 10038

All rights reserved
Printed in the United States of America

ISBN: 978-0-9619518-7-0
ISSN: 2471-5905

Member

Council of Editors of Learned Journals

∞ ™ The paper used in this publication meets the minimum requirements of American National Standard for Information Sciences—Permanence of Paper for printed Library Materials

ANSI Z39.48—1984.

# METHODS
## A JOURNAL OF ACTING PEDAGOGY

EDITORS

SENIOR EDITOR
Ruis Woertendyke	Pace University

ASSOCIATE EDITOR
Charles Grimes	University of North Carolina, Wilmington

PRODUCTION EDITOR
Walter Raubicheck	Pace University

EDITORIAL BOARD
Dr. Lee Evans	Pace University
Dr. David Krasner	Dean College
Lilah Shreeve	Pace University
Laurence Ruth	Pace University
Corey Tazmania	Adjunct @ STNJ, NESF, NSC, NYC, Equity Member Since 2006
Bara Swain	Urban Stages

## Note From the Editor

Now that we have put out a second volume, we've had time to step back and observe our work. The first thing we are struck by is the realization that our articles and book reviews are entirely dependent on the quality of the writers who submit their work for our consideration. We've done well so far and are excited by the diversity of the writers and their varying ideas about acting and theatre.

We have received a number of articles prophesying new approaches to acting, which we are excited to read and understand. These new, modern, approaches promise to expand and redefine acting for the twenty-first century. We embrace these new approaches, as long as they do not diminish the value of the great masters. We don't need to hear about the failures of Stanislavski, Strasberg, Meisner, Adler, and others to appreciate the new methods that have been found to be effective in the 21st century. We want to understand and appreciate these new approaches in their own light and let time make the historical comparisons.

Though the subjects of this second volume are more diverse than those of the first, we want to expand our focus even further in the future by including critical reviews of currently working actors, acting in devised pieces, and histories of well-known actors.

*Methods* is just beginning to serve its purpose. Not long after receiving Sally Bailey and Paige Dickinson's "The Importance of Safely De-roling," I got a call from the young actor playing Helena in my production of John Osborne's *Look Back in Anger*. She told me that she felt guilty and ashamed because of the nature of Helena's role in the play. After her next performance, I followed the de-roling advice in Dickinson and Bailey's article for the entire cast and my Helena thanked me profusely. This is exactly the kind of response we're looking for from the *Methods* articles. One of our key tasks is to become a source for exploring and improving our work with young actors. This is just the beginning.

—R.W.

# TABLE OF CONTENTS

| Author | ARTICLES | Page |
|---|---|---|
| Sally Bailey and Paige Dickinson | The Importance of Safely De-roling | 1 |
| Rebecca Worley | "Walking with Memory": The Pedagogy and Praxis of Embodied Memory | 19 |
| Robert Woods | There's No Business Like Show Business! Teaching the Business of Acting | 41 |
| Cosmin Chivu | An Interview with Zoe Caldwell | 63 |
| David Marcia | The Actress Plays a Man: Making Neil Labute's *Reasons to be Pretty* Strange | 85 |
| Tom Smith | More Than Games: Integrating Improvisation with Stanislavski-based Actor Training | 97 |
| Marjorie Gaines | Theatre as Communication: Performing Arts Training as Foundational Across Disciplines | 111 |
| Lee Evans | Silence is Golden | 119 |

## HISTORY

| | Historical Document | 127 |
|---|---|---|
| Anna Cora Mowatt | *Autobiography of An Actress* | 128 |

## BOOK REVIEWS

| Richard Gilbert | *Stage Combat Arts: An Integrated Approach to Acting* by Christopher DuVal. London: Bloomsbury, 2016. | 139 |

| | | |
|---|---|---|
| Kevin Otos | *The Outstanding Actor: Seven Keys to Success* by Ken Rea. UK: Bloomsbury Methuen Drama, 2015 | 143 |
| Laurel Koerner | *The Actor Training Reader* edited by Mark Evans. UK and New York: Routledge, 2015. | 147 |
| Joel G. Fink | *Acting on the Script* by Bruce Miller. Milwaukee, WI: Applause Theater & Cinema Books, 2014. | 151 |
| Kathleen Mulligan | *The Right to Speak: Working with the Voice*, 2nd ed., by Patsy Rodenburg. London: Bloomsbury, 2015. | 157 |
| Leigh Woods | *Great Shakespeare Actors: Burbage to Branagh* by Stanley Wells. Oxford: Oxford University Press, 2015. | 161 |
| | *Directing Shakespeare in America: Current Practices* by Charles Ney. London: Bloomsbury Arden Press, 2016. | |
| Dennis Schebetta | *The Shakespeare Workbook and Video: A Practical Course for Actors* by David Carey and Rebecca Clark Carey. London, New York: Bloomsbury Methuen Drama, 2015. | 167 |
| Rena Cook | *Acting Shakespeare's Language* by Andy Hinds. London: Oberon Books, 2015. | 173 |
| Jenna Lourenco | *Essential Acting: A Practical Handbook for Actors, Teachers and Directors* by Brigid Panet. New York and London: Routledge, 2009 | 177 |

| Mark Rafael | *Acting with Passion: A Performer's Guide to Emotions on Cue* by Niki Flacks. New York: Bloomsbury Methuen Drama, 2016 | 181 |
| | Notes on Contributors | 187 |
| | Call for Papers, Essays, Book Reviews, and Editors | 195 |

# The Importance of Safely De-roling
*Sally Bailey and Paige Dickinson*

## Introduction

An actor in training spends significant time learning how to grasp and get into a role, but makes virtually no effort learning how to retreat from the role and return to his or her real self once the performance is complete. Getting "stuck" in a role refers to an actor not being able to let go of the character's set of behaviors and to return to oneself. If stuck in negative emotions such as anger, distrust, frustration, or defensiveness, an actor can take home the emotions and personality traits of a particular character and thus put his or her mental and physical health at risk.

Whenever we have presented an introductory workshop about drama therapy as a possible career for theatre majors to college theatre professors, we have been met with surprise when we mentioned the importance of de-roling clients and actors. Professors have generally expressed delight with the concept and have said that for them it is a brand-new idea. In contrast, drama therapists learn the importance of helping clients de-role after improvisations, role-plays, or rehearsals as a matter of course in their training in the United States, Canada and the UK (Cossa; Emunah; Holmwood and Stavrou; Jones; Rule; Sternberg and Garcia).

Drama therapy focuses on role-playing in improvisation, rehearsals, and performances in order to assist clients with the development of new behaviors (often called expanded role repertoire), socio-emotional skills, communication abilities, and self-efficacy, among other positive personal changes. Taking home the personality of a role played out in the therapy session, with its intense emotions, fears, tensions, conflicts, complexities, and anxieties, can leave a client confused as to where one's own boundaries end and the acting role begins. Even if the role is one within the client's current role repertoire (as in the case of playing himself or some aspect of himself), getting "stuck" in a role means that he is not able to let go of that particular set of behaviors and access other roles or parts of the self that might be needed for responding to any given new life situation. A client stuck in anger, distrust, frustration, or defensiveness can act out negatively, or project those residual feelings onto others, even though those feelings may have no connection to the new, unrelated situation. This actually happened to a client living in a drug treatment facility in one of the author's sessions as a young drama therapist. The therapist did not de-role him sufficiently, and when the client left the drama therapy group, he found another resident he did not like and picked a fight with him. That unloaded the uncomfortable feelings he held, but in turn almost got him ejected from the program, a program that does not tolerate violence of any kind among its residents. Likewise, when an actor takes home the emotions and personality traits of a character from rehearsals and performances, his or her own mental and physical health might conceivably be put at risk; the character's tensions, eccentricities, and maladjustments can seep into the actor's personal life.

## The Need for De-roling Techniques

*Problems Created When There is No De-roling*

A number of authorities speak about the "blurred boundaries" that actors face when rehearsing and performing characters (Barton; Burgoyne Dieckman; Burgoyne, Poulin, and Rearden; DeCosta, Buse, and Amdursky; Geer; Rule; Wilson). Having gotten firmly into character with no method for getting out, the actor often takes the character home in both mind and body after leaving rehearsal. In fact, actors who use Stanislavski's system are encouraged to "live oneself into the part," and Method actors, particularly those following Sanford Meisner's version, are encouraged to do much of their affective memory/emotional recall work as "homework" to be completed outside of rehearsal (Carnicke; Krasner). At the very least, the acting process—no matter what acting school it originates from—can lead

# The Importance of Safely De-roling 3

to an actor being "called upon to give up much of his own identity and to suspend temporarily his own boundaries" (Rule 53). After a while an actor might begin to confuse his character's thoughts and feelings with those of his own and begin to have nightmares as his character's life seeps into his subconscious, or feel he is in some way "possessed" by his character (Burgoyne Dieckman; DeCosta *et al*; Rule).

Janice Rule, an actor who underwent psychoanalysis, believes that acting creates recurrent identity crises for actors. She describes an actor friend who took on the cynical attitudes and actual phrases of a character he was performing in a play, and in so doing almost destroyed his engagement to be married. This role confusion was discovered when his fiancée, who was quite hurt by the actor's behavior, glanced at his script and recognized lines and behavior his character expressed in the play that were identical to the phrases and behaviors he was enacting in his own real life (55-56). Later, this same friend went through a similar experience in a film while portraying a soldier on leave with his buddies. In his personal life he started going on drinking benders with his mates in a mirror version of the actions taken by his character. He was totally unaware of "the depth of his unconscious identification with the character," until his wife threatened to leave him (56).

Not de-roling can have physical as well as social and emotional repercussions. A prime example is the case of actor Philip Anglim who, in playing the title role in the original Broadway production of playwright Bernard Pomerance's *The Elephant Man*, developed muscular problems from contorting his body for the role in eight weekly performances. He was well aware of this problem, given that he could not ignore the physical pain that ensued. He took counter measures by soaking his body in Epsom salts, going to the gym to work out, and eventually employing the services of a chiropractor (Smilgis). If he had been alert enough to de-role from the start, he might have implemented a physical and emotional de-roling ritual immediately after each performance in order to prevent muscular problems from developing.

On the plus side, taking the time to de-role promotes positive mental health for actors. De-roling allows actors to leave their characters on stage or in the rehearsal room, where they belong. Aubrey Urban, a former graduate student in acting at Kansas State University, took author Bailey's Principles of Drama Therapy class. When de-roling was first talked about, Aubrey reacted as though a light bulb had been lit. She had never before been introduced to this concept in any of her undergraduate or graduate acting courses, but she immediately grasped the value of it. Later, when she was cast as Lady MacBeth, Aubrey put de-roling to the test. "With Lady MacBeth I had to realize that it was her torment that she was going through and that it had nothing to do with me." Toward the end of the play her character commits suicide onstage by drowning herself, making a deliberate choice to slip into a large well that was a part of the set. Because Aubrey creates her roles through a process of finding the physicality of the character, the minute she disappeared from the audience's view, she began de-roling physically. Backstage she changes the posture and physical tensions of Lady MacBeth in order to start to come back to her true self: "Once I go to curtain call, I accept this as an actor not as the character, because obviously the applause is a celebration of the ensemble that one is a part of, and I want to take that in as myself." Aubrey completed the de-roling process in the dressing room after curtain call, consciously contemplating leaving Lady MacBeth behind as she took off her wig, costume, and makeup while coming back to herself as she put on her own clothing and makeup. "It was very strategic and deliberate when I was taking off my makeup, my costume, my wig, and said 'Good night' to her and I left her in the dressing room." After the show, when author Sally Bailey told her how moved she had been by her performance, Aubrey remarked, "This rehearsal process has been so intense that if I hadn't learned about de-roling from you, I might have committed suicide by now."

# The Importance of Safely De-roling

In a worst-case scenario, without a way of de-roling, actors who have emotional vulnerabilities due to past emotional or physical abuse can face re-traumatization when preparing for and playing a character with a similar or related trauma history. As one former Kansas State undergraduate acting student remarked:

> Acting has never been hard for me because I'm an extremely emotional person, but getting the emotions to cease has always been a challenge of mine. I always would get emotional hang-over. I get in a particular situation where I go back to those [traumatic] memories, and then I would go into this very dark place, and then for the next three or four days it would be just this gloomy cloud hanging over me. It's very physical to me, this cloud of emotion where everything is just hazy, and my memories are quite vague. I would act out and be very hurtful to other people. In an acting class if I was involved in some kind of an exercise, then it might stick with me for a few hours or even an entire day, depending on whether it was a happy role or an extremely depressive one. Depression always stays with me longer than being eccentric and excited. In the musicals and operas I acted in, I was always a very sensual, seductive character which, it would be fair to say fits my personality anyhow . . . it would stick with me a little bit longer, invariably in a negative way. It would de-value my sexuality instead of celebrating it.

## The Prevalence of Trauma in the Lives of Student Actors

The difficulty of de-roling can be magnified, particularly if a beginning actor has had a history of trauma. The previously mentioned undergraduate acting student took a two-week intensive course in Alba Emoting (an approach to guiding emotional states), offered one winter intersession at Kansas State, and she found that whenever she tapped into pure emotion through the effector patterns of basic emotions, she brought back the traumatic memories of her childhood abuse and of a recent on-campus rape. The Step-Out, an Alba Emoting de-roling technique to take the body back to neutral, did not work for her, and furthermore she was reticent to talk about her problems in class discussions because she did not want to be the focus or to turn the class into a therapy group. She does not label those traumatic memories as "flashbacks," but we suspect that they were, since she reports that she was "right back there in that moment."

The U.S Department of Justice (Karjane *et al.* 2005: 2) and the Centers for Disease Control (Black *et al.* 1) both estimate that one-fifth (20%) of women 24 years of age and younger have been raped. This one-out-of-five ratio comprises 79.6% of all lifetime female rape survivors (Black *et al.* 2). Forty-two percent of all female rape survivors were raped before they were 18, that is, before they even arrived at college (Black *et al.* 2). Researchers believe that college-aged women are at an elevated risk for rape compared to women of similar age in the general population, "due to the close daily interaction between men and women in a range of social situations experienced in university settings as well as frequent exposure to alcohol and other drugs" (Krebs *et al.* 1).

Ozer and Weiss estimate that 50% of Americans will experience some type of traumatic experience in their lifetimes, but only about 15-20% ever develop post-traumatic stress disorder (169). Women are twice as likely as men to develop PTSD, in part because they are at higher risk for rape and other sexual victimization (Ozer and Weiss 169). A 2002 National Institute of Justice Report says, "Nearly a third of all rape victims develop rape-related post-traumatic stress disorder at some point in their lives" (Karjane et al. 5).

Awareness of this information is crucial for all secondary and post-secondary school acting instructors, not because they should take on the role of therapist, social worker, or counselor for students who have experienced trauma, but so that they can prevent re-traumatizing anyone in their classes who may be vulnerable. Anecdotal data suggest that typically over half of the students in acting classes are female. Even though there are usually more roles in plays for men, women nevertheless seem to be more drawn to studying theatre, an art form that focuses on expressing feelings. In high school and college, a possibility exists that in any given acting class as many as one quarter of the class might have experienced a sexual trauma such as rape and thus might be vulnerable to a flashback or other symptoms of post-traumatic stress disorder, such as dissociation, emotional numbing (also called anhedonia, a symptom of depression characterized by the inability to feel or experience pleasure), panic attacks, suicidal tendencies, sleep disorders, eating disorders, etc., if they connect deeply with fear, sadness, or anger when they portray a traumatized character in a scene. De-roling after a scene would help mitigate this problem.

However, one does not have to have to be diagnosed with PTSD to have a negative experience with getting "stuck" in a role. Adolescence is often a time when young people first discover their love for theatre and performing. With the intensity and enthusiasm that is so characteristic of teenagers, young acting students are often willing to do whatever a director tells them to do with no protest, especially when auditioning for a part or exploring an "on-the-edge" character. In fact, an actor blindly following a director can be considered a badge of courage and a demonstration of commitment to the dramatic art. This article's co-author, Paige Dickinson, was never traumatized growing up, but she was a very sensitive, emotional adolescent, devoted to the arts, and was able to use her imagination to visualize characters she had read about or had portrayed in plays. She discovered that she had a talent for slipping deeply into a character's emotional and physical life.

When Dickinson was about fourteen years of age, she attended a summer theatre program that provided acting classes and that produced a variety of workshop productions. When it came time to cast the shows, the directors held group auditions. They had everyone lie down on the floor and guided them to en-role in a sequence of characters, asking the students to think about the characters' physicality, personalities, emotions, thought processes, life experiences, and reactions to those life experiences. There was no time taken at the end of one such portrayal to "get out" of the role, before immediately moving on to the next one. The third or fourth character was depressed and sullen. The directors evidently wanted each actor to get into the emotional space of the role and feel the weight of the concerns and burdens that had occurred. As Dickinson tells it:

> They walked us through what they called 'the heavy box' to feel the pressure of the role. It was almost kind of a meditative trance, walking you through a visualization of seeing a really, really heavy box and bringing it towards you and laying it on your chest, so you got the physicality, not just the characteristics of the role. And then the directors said, 'OK, take a minute and we're going to go to the next one.' And that's how they left it! Well, about half the people could not move – literally physically could not move. They began sobbing hysterically, because they were stuck in this extremely dark place. One girl was in a fetal position, sobbing. There were probably three or four students who were in the seventeen to eighteen year old range who really just never came out of it for the balance of the summer program. They had been transformed.

Dickinson reports that the directors did not say or do anything to help the "stuck" students get out of the role; instead they took the unaffected students to the next room and continued the character inductions. They told the "stuck" students, including Dickinson, to join them whenever they felt they were ready. Not one of the directors stayed with the group of upset students in order to make certain they were all right. It took 20 or 30 minutes before most of those left behind felt calm enough to rejoin the group. If Dickinson had known then what she knows now about de-roling, she might well have quickly fixed the entire problem.

## How to De-Role from a Character

De-roling is not a "one size fits all" technique; there are many ways of accomplishing this goal. Sometimes it is very easy to get out of character, while at other times it is more difficult. Sometimes the difficulty has to do with the qualities of the character in relation to the personality of the actor. Sometimes it has to do with where the actor is emotionally after a particular rehearsal or performance. Having a variety of techniques to choose from allows the director/teacher to match the technique to the specific actor, role, and situation. Of course, the ideal is to teach young actors the concept of de-roling and the many ways of doing it, so that actors can begin to take responsibility for finding appropriate ways to de-role themselves as they move into the professional world. Self-care is as important for actors as it is for any other professional who puts their heart on the line in the course of the job.

### *The Step-Out*

Alba Emoting psychologist Susana Bloch created an emotional de-roling technique for her Alba Emoting emotion induction method (Conrad). Alba Emoting was originally developed to help researchers understand what happens physically to the body when certain emotions are felt, by providing a safe and ethical way to induce emotions into research subjects. Bloch discovered four unique effector patterns involving breathing, posture, tension, and facial expressions that induce six basic emotions: anger, sadness, fear, tenderness, joy, and erotic love. Bloch believes that all other emotions come from different intensities and mixtures of these six (Conrad). Because of its proven effectiveness, Alba Emoting has been adopted by a number of European theatre companies. With Alba Emoting, real emotions are generated solely through physical manipulations; actors do not need to use their personal emotional memories to create their characters' emotions as called for by the Method taught by Strasberg, Adler, and Meisner (Conrad; Krasner).

Bloch calls her de-roling technique The Step-Out. It consists of a series of slow, deep breaths synchronized with sweeping arm motions that are begun from a forward bend position with arms above the head, hands clasped, to above and behind the head and then forward again. The actor breathes in while standing and bending backward, then breathes out and bends forward. This takes the actor back to a neutral emotional and physical state. As Bloch says, sounding much like the ethical scientist that she is, "Since one has activated the network, one is de-activating the network" (as cited in Geer 152). Theatre director Richard Owen Geer writes, "step-out works best for those who practice it regularly as part of their training in Alba Emoting" (Geer 153). However, Geer found that actors who were trained in other systems had difficulty leaving all the induced emotions behind using The Step-Out.

### Shifting Spaces and The Dress Shop

Paige Dickinson learned about de-roling when she attended the Cincinnati School for Creative and Performing Arts. Her acting teacher Luther Goins was a professional actor from Chicago. He did not talk about de-roling per se, but talked to each student about identifying what "space" he or she was in. He would ask, "Are you in the stage space or are you in the audience space?" and "Are you in the character's space or are you in your personal space?" Ultimately this process taught students to identify when they were in role and when they were not, and they thus learned how to make a clear distinction between the two states. Whenever they finished working on a scene in class or finished performing in a show, the student actor was very conscious about going through a process Goins called "shifting spaces," centered on helping each student to move from one world to the other.

One of Goins's space shifting exercises was known as The Dress Shop. After a rehearsal or a scene in class, he would talk about the figurative costume of the character and have everyone literally pantomime taking it off. In this way the students shifted from the stage

# The Importance of Safely De-roling

space to their own personal space. Goins was specific and individualized in how he taught each actor the best way to make the transition. The first time Dickinson did the Dress Shop process, Goins walked through it with her. Dickinson was portraying a very angry character, and everything about her role was tightened. Her hair was pulled back into a very tight bun. All her clothes were very tight. Goins started by mirroring her, taking her character's physical posture, and then started to change it until the original character was completely gone. Dickinson mirrored his change. The de-roling process for that character ended up being to take her hair down and brush it out to its fullest, not just taking the bun out and dropping her hair, but literally taking a large brush, flipping her hair upside down and brushing it out so it was completely free and seemingly full of air. She made sure the clothes she changed into after the performance were very baggy and loose, so that there was no way she could take any part of the character home with her.

### Separating the Performance Space from the Audience Space

Another way to de-role a group is to make sure that the performance space is always separated from the audience space both physically and figuratively. When rehearsing in a theatre, while actors are in character, they are onstage. But when the director wants to give notes, the actors need to go back to themselves in order to take in and process the notes. For notes and cast meetings, the actors should sit in the audience area or go to another room. This makes the stage space the only place where the actors are in character. When the actor is on stage, the director can address him or her by the character's name, but when the actor is off stage, the director should use the actor's actual name. This creates another clear separation for the actor between "being in character" and "being myself."

When leading a class or rehearsal in a room, the director/teacher needs to keep the performance space and audience space separate as well. For very young actors, tape should be put on the floor to define the acting area so the practice of crossing the line where on one side the actor is the character and on the other side the actor is him or herself. Be clear when discussing work to refer to the character's emotions and motivations as belonging to the character, not to the actor. It can be easy to blur the two, as the actor is using his or her own body and emotions to bring the character to life. The director/teacher needs to always speak in such as way as to keep the actor and character separate entities in his mind as well as in the minds of the actor and the other cast members.

### Ritual Beginnings and Endings

One way to create a ritual around en-roling and de-roling is to use the opening and closing ritual that drama therapists who practice Developmental Transformations use. At the beginning of a group, everyone stands in a circle and together says, "Bring down [or hum down] the drama therapy curtain [or box]," as they reach up toward the ceiling and pull an imaginary curtain, or box, down to the floor. Then everyone steps inside the imaginary curtain to enter the play space. If a box is pulled down, everyone reaches into the box and pulls out an imaginary costume or imaginary prop. At the end, everyone stands in a circle again and says in unison, "Pull up [or hum up] the drama therapy curtain [or box]," as they pantomime pulling the drawstrings of a curtain or pushing a box up into the ceiling. Simultaneously, they are putting their roles and imaginations away until the next time. It is very easy to remove "therapy" from the statement and just say, "Bring down the drama curtain or the 'curtain of imagination'" and "Pull up the drama curtain or the 'curtain of imagination.'" This creates a very clear demarcation between being involved in the real world and of being in the world of dramatic imagination.

In a similar manner, a director/teacher could use the "space shifting" metaphor that Luther Goins used, asking actors "where" they are at any given time:

- Are you in the stage space or are you in the audience space?
- Are you in the onstage space or the offstage space?
- Are you in the character's space or in your personal space?

## The Importance of Safely De-roling

*Reclaiming Your Name and Your Identity*

One simple de-roling technique is for the actor to reclaim his or her name at the end of rehearsal or at the end of the show. For instance, if an actor named Sandra Miller is playing Blanche DuBois in *A Streetcar Named Desire*, she can say, "I am no longer Blanche! I am Sandra Miller!" To make it more effective, the actor can throw the character off while saying, "I am taking off Blanche and leaving her here! I am now back to being myself! I am Sandra Miller!"

Sometimes one needs more than a change of names to go back to one's own identity. In this case the actor can think of a number of ways in which she is different from the character she is playing. For instance, "Blanche is an alcoholic—I only drink on special occasions. Blanche is very dependent on other people—I am independent and do things on my own! Blanche is passive and I am dynamic!"

To add movement and differentiate space, actors stand in a circle and one by one take turns de-roling. When the actor is speaking about the character, she turns toward the inside of the circle. When the actor is speaking about herself, she turns toward the outside the circle. At the end of the ritual, all of the actors can say "Goodbye [insert name of character]," turn toward the outside of the circle and stride away with energy. The director can end the ritual by saying, "Good night, actors! See you tomorrow!"

*Taking Off the Character*

A simple method of physically getting out of a character is to literally shake it off while vocalizing with an open sound. This loosens the muscles, changes the posture, and physically makes a break from the physicality of the character. Once the muscles change—especially if they loosen and relax—the emotions will automatically change (remember those six effector patterns identified by Susana Bloch).

If shaking off the character is not enough, actors can imagine that there is a giant zipper from the top of their head to the bottom of their toes, unzip the character, and step out of it. Be sure to kick the character's body away—or carefully fold it up and put it away in an imaginary box. We do not recommend putting the character's imaginary body into a pocket or taking it home. Leave it in the theater or classroom space. This is where it is supposed to be until it is brought to life in the next rehearsal or performance.

If the character seems to have a strong "grip" on an actor, other actors can pantomime peeling the character off the actor. The helpers can make this peeling action as simple or difficult as they want depending on how much they sense the actor needs in order to feel de-roled and released from the character. Again, the actor should not take the character's "skin" with him, but leave it in the space.

If there is access to soft fabric or towels, the actors can "wash" the character off themselves or others in the group. One of the authors has even used an imaginary fire hose to thoroughly pressure wash a character off an actor.

Sometimes after a very intense rehearsal, a "Character Washing Machine" works wonders. Cast members line up facing each other in two lines to create the walls of the machine and engage in "cleaning" actions and sounds similar to those heard in a car wash. Each actor takes a turn going through the machine to have his character washed off. Entering the machine the actor would be in character and by the time he left the machine, the character would be gone. As actors leave the machine and return to themselves, they can substitute for different people in the machine wall so that everyone can go through and get their character "washed off."

## Creating and Embodying a Friend

Actor Aubrey Urban has developed a way of seeing the character she is creating in rehearsal as a friend she is getting to know. She goes carefully through the character's history and slowly begins to develop a relationship – finding out what parts of the character are similar to her real self and what parts are different. By the time she is ready for a performance, she says, "I get to embody her for a couple of hours and then I go back to myself. I know she's here, and she's my buddy, but she's not coming home with me, and I'm not adopting her in my soul." To get into character each night she consciously puts on her makeup, costume and wig, reminding herself that she is taking on the embodiment of her friend, in order to allow her to experience life for several hours on the stage. Then, after the show, she reverses the process. "When it's the end of the night, I have to treat it as if I am taking off that character." She takes the time to consciously and methodically transform back into her real self. She often literally says "Goodbye" to the character until the next performance.

*Using Art to De-role*

Sometimes, when letting go of a character is difficult, art helps to facilitate the process. Shannon Garretson, a graduate drama therapy student at Kansas State, used art when she was directing *Almost*, a non-fiction play she had written based on interviews with women who had had abortions. Some of the cast had also had abortions, and they had a variety of feelings about those experiences. By contrast, some of the cast had not had abortions. Some of the cast had strong religious or moral convictions against abortion, while some believed in a woman's right to choose. Shannon wanted to be sure that the actors left their characters, who all had harrowing stories, back in rehearsal, so they did not take the issues of the play home with them and ruminate on them. On a number of evenings she found that the actors had so deeply internalized their characters that in order to de-role, she needed to employ a technique that would reach deeply inside. She gave each person a piece of white paper with a large, empty circle drawn on it. The actors used colored markers to draw a mandala within the circle. Mandalas (Hindu or Buddhist graphic symbols of the universe) are very useful for non-verbally processing and expressing unconscious feelings. Drawing one after an intense rehearsal allowed those feelings to be brought up from the unconscious and to be consciously expressed and released. The actors would leave their mandalas in the rehearsal space. Shannon did not allow the drawings to be taken home until after the show had ended.

## Symbolic Props and Costumes

Mario Cossa shares another ritual for de-roling in his book *Rebels with a Cause: Working with Adolescents Using Action Techniques*. He suggests using a prop or costume piece that has a strong emotional attachment to the character as a surrogate and endow it with the role for the actor. For example, the actor could hold a scarf used in the play and say, "I leave the role of Antigone with this scarf." Then the actor would hand the scarf to the director/teacher, who takes it away from the group and shakes the role out. This ritual de-roles both the actor and the object at the same time. A de-roling process like this might not be important when working on a play where one wants the props and costumes to carry the essence of the performance throughout rehearsals and performances; however, it could be very important to de-role props, scarves, and costume pieces used in a classroom situation where they will be involved in a variety of scenes or improvisations over time. Acting tools need to be freed of emotional associations for the group, so that the tools can go back to being neutral and take on new projections in another scene or class period.

## Conclusion

De-roling is a vital part of acting that has been neglected by modern acting methods. Because of this, the value of learning to get out of role is not appreciated in terms of safety and personal mental health. De-roling should be taught to young actors even in early creative drama classes; doing so would help people understand the difference between the real and the imaginary – an important ability in this day of "docu-dramas" and "reality TV." Including de-roling in adolescent actor training adds an important aspect of self-control and empowerment for young people who are just learning who they are and how to handle the many emotions they possess. Including de-roling in actor training at the college and professional level allows actors to clearly separate their work life from their home life and allows their personality to continue individuating as an adult. Most important, adding knowledge of this small but critical aspect of actor training might save many acting students and professionals from unnecessary traumatization.

## Works Cited

Barton, Robert. "Therapy and actor training." *Theatre Topics* 4.2 (1994): 105-18. Print.

Black, Michelle C., Kathleen C. Basile, Matthew J. Breiding, Sharon G. Smith, Mikel L. Walters, Melissa T. Merrick, Jieru Chen, and Mark R. Stevens. *The National Intimate Partner and Sexual Violence Survey: 2010 Summary Report*. Washington, DC: Centers for Disease Control and Prevention, National Center for Injury Prevention and Control, Division of Violence Prevention. Cdc.gov/Violence Prevention, November 2011. Web. 28 June 2012.

Burgoyne Dieckman, Suzanne. "A Crucible for Actors: Questions of Directorial Ethics." *Theatre Topics*, 1.1 (1991): 1-12. Print.

Burgoyne, Suzanne, Karen Poulin, and Ashley Rearden. "The Impact of Acting on Student Actors: Boundary Blurring, Growth, and Emotional Distress." *Theatre Topics*, 9.2 (1999): 157-179. Print.

Carnicke, Sharon Marie. "Stanislavsky's System: Pathways for the Actor." Ed. Alison Hodge. *Twentieth Century Actor Training*. London: Routledge, 2000.11-36. Print.

Conrad, Hyrum, ed. *The Development of Alba Emoting: The Work of Dr. Susana Bloch and Collaborators*. Idaho: Brigham Young University, 2003. Print.

Cossa, Mario. *Rebels with a Cause: Working with Adolescents Using Action Techniques*. London: Jessica Kingsley Publishers, 2006. Print.

DeCosta, Louise, William Buse, and Audrey Amdursky. "Personal Myths: Living Them and Pretending Them: Ways in Which Three Actors' Theatrical Lives Reveal the Part Personal Myths Play in Human Functioning." *Dynamic Psychotherapy* 4.2 (1986): 131-139. Print.

Emunah, Renee. "From Adolescent Trauma to Adolescent Drama: Group Drama Therapy with Emotionally Disturbed Youth." Ed. Sue Jennings *Dramatherapy with Children and Adolescents*. London: Routledge, 1995. 150-168. Print.

Geer, Richard Owen. "Dealing with Emotional Hangover: Cool-down and the Performance Cycle in Acting. *Theatre Topics* 3.2 (1993): 147-158. Print.

Hines, Denise A., Jessica L. Armstrong, Kathleen Palm Reed, and Amy Y. Cameron. "Gender Differences in Sexual Assault Victimization Among College Students." *Violence and Victims*. 27.2 (2012): 922-940. Print.

Holmwood, Clive, and Carla Stavrou. "Dramatherapy and Drama Teaching in School – A New Perspective: Towards a Working Relationship." Eds. Laurine Leigh, Irvine

Gersch, Ann Dix, and Deborah Haythorne. *Dramatherapy with Children, Young People, and Schools: Enabling Creativity, Sociability, Communication and Learning.* London: Jessica Kingsley Publishers, 2012. 30-38. Print.

Jones, Phil. *Drama as Therapy: Theory, Practice and Research.* 2nd Ed. London: Routledge, 2007. Print.

Krasner, David. "Strasberg, Adler and Meisner: Method Acting." Ed. Alison Hodge. *Twentieth Century Actor Training.* London: Routledge, 2000. 129-150. Print.

Karjane, Heather M., Bonnie S. Fisher, and Francis T. Cullen. *Campus Sexual Assault: How America's Institutions of Higher Education Respond.* Washington, DC: U.S. Department of Justice, Office of Justice Programs, National Institute of Justice, October 2002. Web. 29 June 2012.

---. *Sexual Assault on Campus: What Colleges and Universities Are Doing About It.* Washington, DC:U.S. Department of Justice, Office of Justice Programs, National Institute of Justice, December 2005. Web. 28 June 2012.

Krebs, Christopher P., Christine H. Lindquist, Tara D. Warner, Bonnie S. Fisher, and Sandra L. Martin. *The Campus Assault Study.* Washington, D.C.: Department ofJustice, Office of Justice Programs, National Institute of Justice, December 2007. Web. 28, June 2012.

Ozer, Emily J. and Daniel S. Weiss. "Who Develops Post Traumatic Stress Disorder?"*Current Direction in Psychological Science.* 13.4 (2004): 169-172. Print.

Pino, Nathan W., and Robert F. Meier. "Gender Differences in Rape Reporting." *SexRoles* 40 (1999): 979-990. Print.

Rule, Janice. "The Actor's Identity Crises (Postanalytic Reflections of an Actress)." *International Journal of Psychoanalytic Psychotherapy* 2.1 (1973): 51-76. Print.

Smilgis, Martha. "Philip Anglim Had To Go Through Contortions To Import And Star In *The Elephant Man.*" *People* 2.24 People Archive, 10 December 1979. Web 20 March 2012.

Sternberg, Patricia, and Antonina Garcia. *Sociodrama: Who's in Your Shoes?* 2nd Ed. Westport: CT: Praeger, 2000. Print.

Undergraduate Acting Student at K-State. Personal interview. 20 March 2012.

United States Department of Justice. "Sexual Violence." *Engaging Communities. Empowering Victims. Section 6: Statistical Overviews. 2015 National Crime Victim's Rights Week Resource Guide.* Office of Justice Programs. Office for Victims of Crime, 2015: 59-63.Web. 28 December 2015.

Urban, Audrey. Personal interview. 19 March 2012.

"What is PTSD?" PTSD Alliance. Web. 27, December 2015.

Wilson, Glenn D. *Psychology for Performing Artists: Butterflies and Bouquets.* London: Jessica Kingsley Publishers, 1994. Print.

# "Walking with Memory": The Pedagogy and Praxis of Embodied Memory

*Rebecca Worley*

> "The act of memory is a physical act and lies at the heart of the art of the theatre. If the theatre were a verb, it would be 'to remember.'"
> —Anne Bogart, *A Director Prepares*

## Proposing a Methodology: The Mind-Body Connection

The act of walking is something that has been considered, utilized, and explored by philosophers, writers, naturalists, and artists. Walking is seen as a political act of protest, a vehicle for health and fitness, or a sign of leisure. More importantly, "walking shares with making and working that crucial element of engagement of the body and the mind with the world, of knowing the world through the body and the body through the world" (Solnit 29). *The Stanford Encyclopedia of Philosophy* defines memory as "one of the most important ways by which our histories animate our current actions and experiences" (Sutton). Michel de Certeau states that memory "sustains itself by *believing* in the existence of possibilities and by vigilantly awaiting them, constantly on the watch for their appearance" (87). Memory, then, is a container for past events and can shape our personal identity. That memory affects the ways in which humans engage with and move in the world is a phenomenon full of potential and possibility.

The act of walking can, when aligned with the mind, take on far more aesthetic and creative meanings than merely an act of moving from one space to another. In this paper, I propose a methodology for aligning the body and the mind via the act of walking as a way to embody memory and emotion. For purposes of this methodology, the terms walking and movement are used interchangeably. It is necessary to note that the term "walking" refers to the ways in which people move through the world, however that concept may manifest itself. This methodology does not, in any way, inhibit or exclude differently-abled bodies. In traditional theater practices, this methodology can be used as a warm-up technique, a character exploration, and a performance.

While this practice focuses primarily upon process over product, its application in both warm-up technique and character exploration and development is intended for use with an eye toward outcome. In my exploration of embodied memory through walking as a pedagogical and methodological approach to performance, I draw from a number of experiences in which I utilize the process, including workshop environments, rehearsal processes, and performance experiments. Here I incorporate my personal encounters with this approach as well as feedback from participants and observers of a performance.

This methodology, which I call "Walking with Memory," takes its inspiration from well-known theater practices and theories such as Augusto Boal's physical theater, Anne Bogart's Viewpoints and Laban's Continuum of Efforts. I also borrow from Yve-Alain Bois and Rosalind E. Krauss's response to Georges Bataille's *informe* and modern art, *Formless: A User's Guide*, in which the authors propose to address and dispel postulates of art they view as little more than myths. I am particularly interested in and inspired by the authors' confrontation of Postulate 4: that "the modernist ontology requires an artwork to have a beginning and an end, and holds that all apparent disorder is necessarily reabsorbed in the very fact of being bounded" (26). The operation of Pulse reveals that art—and time—do not have a clear beginning, middle, and end. Instead, one discovers that time is cyclical, particularly when confronting life events—memories—to which we return again and again.

Through the application of this methodology, students will gain tools connecting body and mind through the embodiment of personal memories by way of individual and group exercises, and performers will gain insight into how embodied memory affects our carriage as well as the topographical patterns left behind in our footprints. "Walking with Memory" can also be employed in the process of character development in which the practice allows students to explore and interpret a character external to themselves through their own personal experiences and memories made manifest in walking.

## Tracing the Memory Path: Theories, Practices, and Methodologies

Like all artistic practices, "Walking with Memory" has its own memory and was inspired by well-known theater practices and theories. In order to describe how "Walking with Memory" can be implemented as a pedagogical and methodological approach to performance one must first establish a working understanding of the techniques which inform the method.

Though inspired by practitioners and theories in Physical Theater more than any other form, it is necessary to acknowledge the points of influence and departure from traditional forms of theatre. Uta Hagen's concepts of Emotional Memory and Sense Memory are significant in the exploration of embodied memory; however, there are decisive differences between her theories and "Walking with Memory." Hagen and other Stanislavsky-based acting methodologies champion the inside-out approach to character exploration and development. "Walking with Memory," on the other hand, is neither from the inside-out nor from the outside-in. Instead, internal and external conditions are concurrent, cyclical, and imbricated. One's pattern of movement is both affected by and simultaneously affecting memories and emotion.

In *Respect for Acting*, Hagen separates Emotional Memory from Sense Memory stating that Emotional Memory is the "recall of a psychological or emotional response" whereas Sense Memory "deals with physiological sensations" (46). In exploring memory and emotion, I do not differentiate between the two techniques. Instead, I find it beneficial to explore memory through the five senses, asking questions such as "If this memory was a color, what is it?" and "If this memory was a scent, what does it smell like?" Approaching concrete descriptions of memories using an abstract lens frequently helps direct performers toward a more fully embodied experience. Finally, I differ from Hagen in that she believes Emotional Memory "deals with the problem of finding a substitution in order to release that big burst of tears, the shriek of terror, the fit of laughter" (46). Exploration of memory via the act of walking does not necessarily require responses of the magnitude described by Hagen. Like Hagen, I believe it is crucial to stress that "Walking with Memory" is not theater as therapy. Although the method draws upon personal memories, it is of utmost importance that the actor avoid any experience not yet comprehended or not yet gained an objective distance from.

As a director, I utilized Anne Bogart's Viewpoints when staging productions to ignite my imagination, as well as the imagination of my actors, and build ensemble. Of the nine Viewpoints of Time and Space, I employ Tempo, Duration, Kinesthetic Response, Shape, Gesture, Spatial Relationship, and Topography. While I stay true to Bogart's definition of the terms, I have developed my own interpretation of Kinesthetic Response. Bogart defines this term as the spontaneous reaction to stimuli outside of the self, as well as "the timing in which you respond to the external events of movement or sound" (8). I define Kinesthetic Response as the manner in which our internal energies (memories, thoughts, and emotions) respond as we encounter external forces, which can be sound or motion but also the internal/external energies of others.

According to Barbara Adrian in the Introduction to her text *Actor Training the Laban Way*, Laban developed his Continuum of Efforts (hereafter referred to as "Efforts") in order to provide a system of analysis for changes in movement. Efforts refers to the way movement is carried out with respect to inner intention. The Efforts are *Time, Space, Weight,* and *Flow.* In many ways, the Continuum of Efforts resembles Bogart's Viewpoints in that they also explore action through time and space.

Other forms of Physical Theater served as influential sources for "Walking with Memory," including Boal's Image Theater in which ideas are enacted visually using tableaux and statues to express and embody emotions, scenarios, and concepts that might have different meanings for different people. Boal's *Games for Actors and Non-Actors* provides a number of games and exercises that guide performers toward a greater understanding of the ways in which the mind-body connection can be implemented as a methodology.

In addition to theatrical influences, "Walking with Memory" engages non-theatre sources such as Bois and Krauss's *Formless: A User's Guide*. In their Postulate 4, the authors use the operation of Pulse to question linear temporality. Pulse attacks the supposition that time has a clear beginning, middle, and end and "presupposes an initial order and a deterioration of that order" (Bois and Kraus 34-36). In her entry on Pulse, Krauss addresses Freud's treatment of repetition stating "Freud began to theorize the structure through which a patient is doomed to the compulsive repetition of an event, particularly an event which, far from pleasurable, is an extreme source of anxiety and terror" (163-64). Krauss goes on to state that "this, then, is the rhythm of shock" (164). Pulse is the afterimage left on the mind's eye after the flash of light; it is rhythm of life and death, emotion, and movement. Pulse is the ancient sense of memory "which designates a presence to the plurality of times and is thus not limited to the past" (de Certeau 218) but continues to manifest itself in the present and affect the future.

The final pertinent practice in "Walking with Memory" is walking meditation. Drawn primarily from Buddhist practices, walking meditation seeks to bring the practitioner to mindful awareness. According to Robert Aitken in the Introduction to Thich Nhat Hanh's *A Guide to Walking Meditation*, mindful awareness "begins with the self, with an understanding of what is happening within, and also out there in the world" (2). Like Bogart's Topography, walking meditation asks that one "consciously make an imprint on the ground with each step" (Hanh, Walking Meditation 16). Practitioners of walking meditation believe that breath is the link between mind and body. As one's breath synchronizes with their steps, thoughts are better directed and mindful awareness is increased. In "Walking with Memory," I encourage an awareness of the influence memories and actions have on breathing patterns, as well as the ways in which breath is engaged to control and manipulate emotion.

## "Walking with Memory": A Pedagogical Tool

"Walking with Memory" can be used in both the classroom and in workshop scenarios in order to guide students toward an understanding of how our internal state-of-being directly affects the manner in which we carry ourselves. Memories of significant people or moments in our lives evoke emotions that change our movement patterns, eye contact, facial expressions, and our relationship to our environment and those within its confines. It is paramount that students not lose themselves in the past; they must draw from their history while simultaneously maintaining an awareness of how that past influences their present state of being both physically and mentally. Our past and our memories can serve as endless resources for physical and mental self-awareness, as well as artistic practices. Human experience in performance is "alchemy" (Bogart, *A Director Prepares* 104).

### Exercise One – Walking as Yourself

**Overview:** The purpose of this exercise is to increase physical and mental self-awareness. If a performer is aware of his or her natural movements and habits, as well as the effect of their mental state-of-being on their physical being, they are better able to control and manipulate their minds and bodies, leading to a wider range of choices and freedom in character exploration and development. In a workshop scenario, where time is often limited, it is best to begin with this type of exercise. In the classroom or rehearsal process, this exercise can serve as a warm-up.

**The Exercise:** Students begin by moving throughout the space at a medium pace. Once the instructor feels that all students have achieved the optimal state of internal focus (usually reached in one to two minutes), they may begin side coaching.

1. What is your natural *leading center*? Is it your chest? Your chin, shoulders, stomach? ("Leading Center" is a concept developed by Delsarte and simply refers to the area of the body from which movement originates. It is also referred to as *Initiation* by Laban.)

2. How does the rest of your body respond to and follow this leading center? What happens to your spine? How do your arms respond? Your hands? What are your shoulders doing? How do your muscles feel? Are they relaxed or tense? Where do you feel tension?

3. What is your breathing pattern? Are you taking deep breaths or shallow ones? Are you breathing rapidly? Is your breathing pattern slow and relaxed? Are you breathing through your nose or through your mouth? How does this affect your breathing?

4. What is your Tempo? What is your Duration? How fast or slow are you moving? How long do you take between steps? What is the Weight of your steps? How strong (heavy) or light are they? It can be useful to clap out rhythms to illustrate possible tempo/rhythms.

5. What is your Topography? If there were paint on the bottom of your feet, what color would it be? What pattern would you leave behind? Would they be scuffed because you drag your feet? Do you walk on the balls of your feet? On the sides? What part of your foot meets the floor first? Do you walk in a "heel-toe" pattern or a "toe-heel" pattern? Are your steps very close together or are they far apart? How do your shoes (if you are wearing them) alter your walking pattern? Do you walk in straight lines, curves, or a zig-zag pattern?

   a. Note: depending on the space and resources, this can be done as an activity by itself and with real paint (I suggest tempera paint) in order to leave visible evidence of topography.

   b. In addition to topography, this series of questions also incorporates the Efforts of Space (direct or indirect movement), Weight, and Flow. When all performers' topography is considered as a whole, the Viewpoint of Spatial Relationship is also applied.

6. What is your *Kinesthetic Response* when you encounter others? Where do your eyes focus? Do you look at the floor, the ceiling, or directly in front of you? What kind of eye contact to you make? Does your facial expression change when you encounter others? How does your topography change? Do you move around others when you cross paths or do you expect them to move for you? How does your tempo adjust in relation to those around you? Do you speed up or slow down? Does your breathing pattern change? This series of questions also integrates the Viewpoints of Shape, and Spatial Relationship and the Efforts of Time, Space, and Flow.

7. What emotions do you feel? How do these emotions influence your posture and your movement?

**Feedback:** After exploring the above questions, I encourage taking at least five minutes for a feedback session. Ask the students what they have discovered about themselves, beginning with their leading center, giving them time to describe how it affected the rest of their body. It is important to ask the students if they were aware of their natural habits (posture, walking patterns, eye contact, etc.) prior to this exercise or if they discovered anything not previously known.

In a classroom setting where it is possible to engage in this exercise on multiple days, it is of particular import that the students are guided toward a discovery of how their actions change depending on the day. In this way, the students can gain an understanding of how situations, emotions, and physical/mental states can change the ways in which they move through the world.

### Exercise Two – Changing it Up

**Overview:** Once students are aware of their natural movement patterns and the mind-body connection, they can then begin to manipulate and change their leading center. As the instructor directs them through a variety of leading centers, the students should become aware of how the rest of the body responds to this leading center.

# Walking with Memory

As the students experiment with a changed external presentation, they also begin to explore how those changes affect their internal state of being.

This exercise is excellent for character exploration and development. In the classroom or workshop environment, it can be applied to improvise, explore, and create characters. In the rehearsal process, the performers can, instead, begin with their scripted character and ask questions such as: How does this character move? What is the leading center? In this way, they can experiment with an outside-in approach to developing the character they are playing.

**The Exercise:** Begin in the same way as Exercise One, allowing the students to move throughout the space as themselves. The instructor should give enough time between each question for play and discovery.

  1. Once you feel you have determined your leading center, I am going to ask that you change it. I will give specific body parts to explore as a leading center. Pay attention to how the rest of your body adjusts. How you interpret each leading center is up to you. Do not worry if your interpretation is different from those around you. Be creative and make bold choices.

  2. Move with your _____ as your leading center.

   a. Note: I usually start with something simple like the right shoulder, nose, or chin. After exploring a number of simple leading centers, I then incorporate more complicated centers such as a knee, an ear, or a foot.

   b. Once the students have established the leading center, guide them through the same questions listed in Exercise One (re: how does the rest of the body adjust?)

  3. What images come to mind? What kind of character type would move in this manner? Where would this character live? What images come to mind? If this character were a color, what would it be? What does this character smell like? If this character were a taste, what would it be? What does this character sound like?

  4. As you encounter others, what is your kinesthetic response?

How does your character interact with them? Are there other characters to or by whom your character is drawn or repelled?

5. What emotions do you feel? Is this character angry, happy, disgusted?

6. What personal memories do you have about this type of character? Does this character remind you of someone specific? A specific situation or scenario?

Continue to change leading centers, asking the above questions with each one. Allow the students enough time to fully explore and discover each leading center and how it affects movement, emotion, and memory.

**Feedback:** The feedback session should be similar to that of Exercise One.

*Exercise Three – Embodying Memory*

**Overview:** The previous exercises take an outside-in approach to physical exploration and character exploration/discovery/creation. When students understand the mind-body connection, they can then reverse the approach and shift to an inside-out approach.

This exercise leads students through memory recall and into an embodiment of that memory. Not only will students explore how memories motivate the ways in which they move through the world but it can also serve to bring the past into the present. For example, if a participant engages an early childhood memory of a parent, they may embody said memory by walking in the teetering, side-to-side manner of small children. A memory of sitting in a hospital waiting room may evoke emotions of anxiousness or anticipation and can manifest itself in restless pacing and fidgeting with clothing or other objects. Younger or inexperienced students may have difficulty moving beyond an internalized or subtle embodiment of their memories. Guide these students toward making bold choices that engage the entire body.

It is necessary to reiterate that this process is not theater as therapy; participants should not use this exercise to work through painful or traumatic memories or experiences. If used in a workshop scenario where the instructor is more likely unfamiliar with the students, it may be best to direct them specifically toward joyful memories. In a classroom or rehearsal setting where there may be more knowledge of the students/performers, there is potential for greater freedom; however, be aware that this exercise can evoke powerful memories and responses. The students' mental and emotional well-being should be considered and respected.

**The Exercise:** Allow the students to find a space in the room where they can sit comfortably and focus. It may prove beneficial to begin with breathing or focus activities before beginning this exercise.

1. Take a moment to think of a memory. It can be a memory about a person or simply about a moment in your past. It should be a strong memory, one that had significant impact on your life.

2. Where does this memory take place? Is it a specific environment (your room) or is it a more generalized location (your hometown)? What is around you in this location? What do you see?

3. When does this memory take place? Is it a specific moment in your life, a day, or a general time-period (when you were little, a summer)?

4. If this memory is about a person, who are/were they to you? What did/do they mean to you? What impact do/did they have on your life?

5. If this memory were a color, what would it be? If it had a smell, what is it? What does it taste like? Sound like?

6. When you have the memory clearly in your mind, begin moving through the space, allowing that memory to inhabit your body fully as you move. If the instructor notes students who are "feeling" the memory more than they are allowing the memory full embodiment, it is acceptable to make statements such as, "Don't be afraid to allow this memory to inhabit your body fully. Make bold choices." Encourage the students to avoid literal interpretations.

7. Does this memory make you dance, skip, float? Does this memory make it difficult to move?

8. What is your leading center? How does the rest of your body respond? What shape does your body take? What gestures are you inspired to make?

9. What is your tempo? Your duration? Are your tempo and duration consistent or varied?

10. What is your topography? Imagine you are leaving the color of your memory imprinted on the floor as you move.

11. What is your breathing pattern? How do the emotions you are experiencing affect your breath?

12. As you encounter others, what is your kinesthetic response? What is your spatial relationship to those around you? Do you need more space? Are you drawn to reach out or be near others? Does their energy influence or change your energy?

**Feedback:** As with the feedback sessions for Exercises One and Two, guide the students through their discoveries. It is not necessary for students to share their memories but it is vital that they are able to discuss how those memories affected their bodies and how they interacted with others during the exercise. Lead the students toward a discussion of how thought and emotional concepts manifested themselves physically.

*Pedagogical Notes: General Comments for the Exercises*

It is best to begin the exercises as quickly as possible in order to engage the students physically and mentally. Depending on time limitations and personal approaches in pedagogy, the instructor may choose to give a brief overview of the terminology and concepts prior to beginning or may prefer to introduce the terminology and concepts during the process. I am in favor of utilizing side-coaching as students execute the exercises. In this way, students are encouraged to maintain a constant self-awareness and engage in self-evaluation during the process. This also helps toward grounding the students in the present, even while embodying memory.

Each question should be posed with enough time in between to allow students the opportunity to discover the answer to what is asked of them. It is also beneficial to provide a list of possible answers as this helps with recognition. Instead of settling on a generic answer, they can be guided toward specificity (i.e. instead of determining their *head* is their leading center, they can pinpoint the exact part of their head: forehead, chin, nose, etc. that acts as their leading center).

There should be no talking or an external focus at the beginning of each activity, as this distracts from the task, and can change the way the students move. It is not until Kinesthetic Response is addressed that students should consciously shift their focus from internal to external. In the second exercise, students may begin vocalizing in the third series of questions and interacting with others in the fourth.

Depending on how large the space and/or the number of participants, it is possible to split the class into two groups (participants and observers) to allow ample room for active participation. This sort of objective distance can be beneficial for the entire class in that multiple perspectives can offer discoveries and observations that would not have been possible otherwise. If the instructor chooses to split the class into two groups, students should have the opportunity to experience both roles during the process.

The benefit of the feedback sessions to the process should not be underestimated. It is imperative that students have the opportunity to verbalize their discoveries in order to continue the self-evaluative process. Relate each question to the others as much as possible (i.e. how did your tempo affect your breathing pattern?). Pay particular attention to the discovery of the mind-body correlation, asking the students to connect their mental/emotional state-of-being with their physical habits.

If the second and third exercises are conducted in a workshop or classroom environment, navigate students toward how they can apply this process in pre-rehearsal/performance warm-ups and in character exploration/discovery when developing scripted characters. If using the third exercise for the exploration of a scripted character in the rehearsal process, it may be beneficial to first use it as a pre-rehearsal warm-up in order to help the performers gain a general understanding of the process. Once in rehearsal, the performers can then incorporate memories of their past that may be analogous to the experiences or situations of their character(s), similar to Hagen's *Substitution*. The memory does not—and probably should not—be an exact translation. Instead, the performer should use a memory that will guide him or her toward a full embodiment of their character in that moment.

### "Walking with Memory": Two Performances

"Walking with Memory" began not as a pedagogical tool for character exploration and development but as a performance art piece. Inspired by the Bois and Krauss text, *Formless*, I determined to create a piece that applied my interpretation of the operations Pulse and Horizontality. Horizontality confronts the notion that art "is addressed to the subject as an erect being, far from the horizontal axis that governs the life of animals . . . [and] presupposes the viewer's having forgotten that his or her feet are in the dirt" (25). Like Bois and Krauss, I too am determined to push against the belief that art is created for viewing on the vertical axis. I had long desired to experiment with Bogart's explanation of topography, wanting to use real instead of imagined paint to make visible the pattern of motion as performers move from place to place on the stage.

While intrigued by the possibility of creating a performance piece inspired by Horizontality, Pulse and Krauss's explanation of trauma as "the rhythm of shock" (164) served as the true impetus for the performance piece. Despite the fact that I had intended to avoid any subject that was deeply personal in my performance piece, I was intrigued by this phrase. Two years before, I lost my father somewhat unexpectedly. During my grieving process, I frequently became lost in memories as I engaged in my daily life. As time passed and I was able to contemplate my grief with distance and clarity, I became cognizant of the fact that memories are a constant pulse—a rhythm—in our lives and influence how we carry ourselves. Considering my own experiences, it occurred to me that people do not comprehend how their walking patterns—their topography—are external manifestations of their internal states-of-being. I wanted to make visible how memories and emotions can change the ways in which we move through the world.

*Performance One – Walking Alone*

The first iteration of "Walking with Memory" as a performance art piece was an experimental solo performance in which I embodied the memories of four phases of my relationship with my father. As this was an independent performance, the memories that I performed were pre-determined. This would change in the second performance. For the piece, I used rolls of brown butcher paper cut to lengths that symbolized the time of each phase. The first and second phases (childhood and young adulthood) were of equal length (roughly eight feet long), while the third phase (the period in which he was dying) was half the length of the previous phases. The fourth phase (my life after his death) remained on the roll in order to symbolize my ongoing experience with the memories of my father. Each phase was represented by a specific paint color. The childhood phase was green to represent growth, nature, and joy. The young adulthood phase was brown and represented the difficult and complicated relationship I had with my father. I used red for the dying phase, which represented the pain and anger I experienced while waiting for him to pass away. The final phase was a combination of all three colors and referenced the fact that I carry all the memories of my father with me each day.

In preparation for the performance, I rehearsed each memory, allowing myself to return mentally to each phase of my life and, in turn, allowing those memories to affect my movement. My childhood relationship with my father was a positive one, connected to nature and endless possibilities. I discovered that my walk for this memory was light, almost a skip, and mostly on the balls of my feet. My tempo was quick and my eyes looked up in admiration and devotion. I could not help but smile, knowing I was safe and happy.

As I grew older, the relationship with my father became much more complicated and distant. It was a relationship dominated by hatred, disdain and, finally, disregard. As I allowed the memories of this phase of our relationship to inhabit my body, I felt heavy and tense. My steps were more of a stomp and it was very difficult to take the next step. My shoulders hunched, curving my spine, as I drew myself inward in a protective and closed posture. I could not look ahead, only down, as my jaw clenched and my breath quickened.

Waiting for my father to pass away was filled with exhaustion and pain. My steps were heavy simply because the amount of energy required to take each one was insurmountable. Nothing seemed real; I felt disconnected from everything around me. While my steps were heavy, the remainder of my body was disjointed and unstable.

In the final phase, I had come to terms with my grief and my anger. As I moved confidently toward my future, my steps were sure, but easy. My experiences had shaped me into the woman I had become and I had accepted them for what they were.

Because I had spent significant time exploring and discovering each walk, I was able to shift seamlessly from one phase to the next during my performance. Between each phase, however, I took a moment to engage in deep, conscious breathing, which centered my mind and body on each memory. With each breath, I allowed the memories of that phase to flood into my mind and inhabit my body. It was imperative to the performance that I did not begin the next walk until my breath and body had fully engaged with each memory.

*Performance Two – Walking with Others*

Following the experimental performance, I wanted to extend the piece in a way that would include the participation of others. In *Relational Aesthetics*, Nicholas Bourriaud states that relational art takes "as its theoretical horizon the realm of human interactions and its social context rather than the assertion of an independent and

# Walking with Memory

*private* symbolic space" (14). Memories are created through human interaction. I wanted to discover how the inclusion of other people in my performance piece would change the topography—the visible traces—of embodied memories.

For the second performance, I wanted to turn my spectators into Boal's spect-actors in order to create a piece that would change as different people chose to engage in the performance as they walked their own memories. Because I intended to invite spectators to walk with me, I did not pre-determine which memories I would embody throughout the entire performance. Instead, I prepared two memory walks in which I "walked with" another family member who had passed away (though each of my performances focused on family members who had passed away, this is in no way a requirement for performance or the methodology. I consciously made the choice to work with these memories for performative reasons). These walks were performed alone in order to establish the concept and then I invited others to join me as I continued to walk. Having prepared only two memory walks allowed for a certain level of spontaneity and openness to and on the part of my fellow performers.

Because this performance was going to include additional participants, I created a surface large enough to accommodate several people walking their memories simultaneously. To allow for a more dynamic visual topography, I provided ten different colors of tempera paint from which the performers could choose.

The performance began with my solo memory walks. As I walked, a PowerPoint slide show was projected on the wall behind me. The slides read:

- Who do we carry with us as we move through life?
- How have our experiences shaped who we are today? Who we will be in the future?
- How do our memories affect the way we move through the world?
- What if these memories made themselves visible?

- What would our memories look like as they left their traces on our footprints as they have our minds and hearts?
- What does it look like when our paths—our memories—cross, meet, come together, part?

The questions, posed to the spectators as I engaged in my solo memory walks, encouraged them to contemplate the questions that had inspired my performance. The slides were timed to allow the execution of two solo walks, after which I invited others to join me in walking their own embodied memories. Prior to the performance, I had arranged with two spectators who agreed to become spect-actors in the performance. It was essential that the pre-arranged spect-actors understood that they should embody their memories however they saw appropriate, whether through dancing, skipping, walking, or remaining still during the performance. This allowed for greater freedom in participants' interpretation and execution of their memory walks.

In addition to the pre-arranged spect-actors, several other spectators chose to participate in and brought their own energy to the performance. As I had hoped, more than one participant embodied their memories in creative ways—some danced, some only put one toe on the edge of the stage, others purposefully walked on and changed the memory topographies of other performers. Though I had begun the piece walking painful memories, I discovered how much the energy of those around me influenced my own energy and, therefore, memories. As the blank, white stage filled with the footsteps of other people's memories, the piece evolved and was forever marked. As we interact with those around us, so too are we forever impacted by their presence and their memory.

### Conclusion: Taking Memory into the Future

Following the performances of "Walking with Memory," I continued to explore the ways in which the concept of embodied memory and emotion could be utilized as a pedagogical and methodological

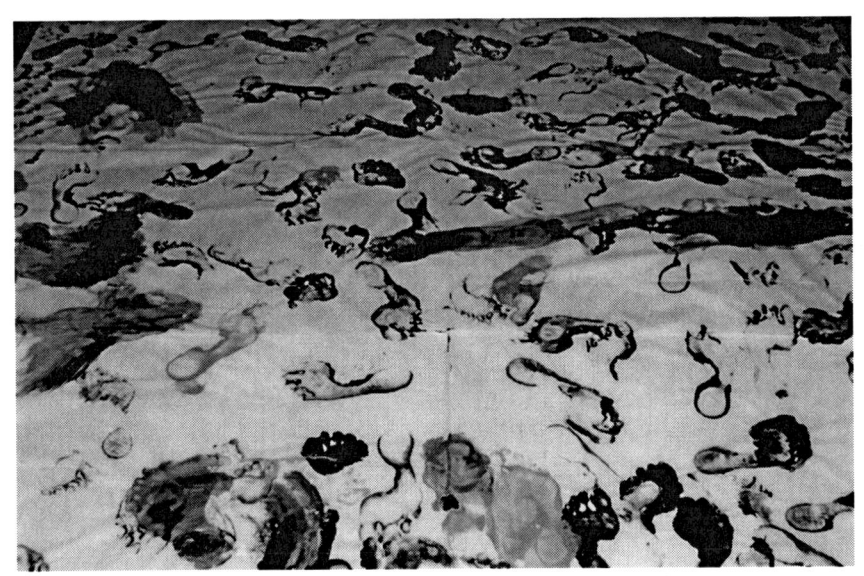

*Photo by Rebecca Worley. See Pace University Press website for four color version.*

approach to performance. My experiences as an actor, a director, and a teacher provided the in-depth understanding of the theories and methodologies that influenced "Walking with Memory." It was not, however, until my personal memories combined with my artistic knowledge that the seed for "Walking with Memory" was planted.

In *A Director Prepares*, Anne Bogart states, "the function of art is to awaken what is asleep. How do you awaken what is asleep? . . . you turn it slightly until it awakens" (53). Theater practitioners and theorists have used emotional memory in character development for a century, yet few look beyond the psychological implications of this technique. When "turned slightly," one discovers the pedagogical and methodological potential of the embodiment of personal memories in the act of walking. Physical theater practitioners have long emphasized the mind-body correlation and their methodologies have proved invaluable to the development of "Walking with Memory." However, Viewpoints and Efforts fail to take full advantage of a performer's personal history, their memories, as a way to explore and develop characters and performance. Embodied memory is the alchemical result of psychological and physical theater practices, out of which has grown a technique that awakens the full potential of our memories and the mind-body connection.

I continue to experiment with "Walking with Memory" as a pedagogical and methodological tool for artistic expression and creation. What I have learned through my performances and while teaching the method is that our memories can serve as powerful sources of inspiration, self-awareness, exploration, and discovery. Embodied memories can also provide a pathway for more profound human relations. During the performance art piece, one spect-actor was cognizant of the recent loss of my family member and recognized that I was walking with memories of him. In the talk-back session following my performance, this spect-actor stated that she felt a certain responsibility to honor my memory path as she did not want to interfere with or disturb that specific memory.

I, too, have become more cognizant of the memory paths others leave behind them as they move throughout their lives. As Solnit states, "The motions of the mind cannot be traced, but those of the feet can" (6). In my experiences with "Walking with Memory," I have come to practice mindful awareness, not just of my own embodied memories, but of those around me as well. When we allow our memories to fill our minds and bodies, when we explore these memories via physical embodiment, we not only open a path between the past and the present that holds great potential for artistic energy and articulation, but we also open the possibility of increased awareness of, and therefore responsibility to, our fellow walkers. "Walking with Memory" has provided me with a way to "know the world through [my] body and [my] body through the world" (Solnit 29) and as I consider my own footsteps as I progress through the world, I cannot help but consider the footprints of others.

## Works Cited

Adrian, Barbara. *Actor Training the Laban Way: An Integrated Approach to Voice, Speech, and Movement.* New York: Allworth, 2008. Print.

Batchelor, Martine. "Meditation and Mindfulness." *Contemporary Buddhism* 12.1 (2011):157164. Academic Search Premier. Web. 31 Mar. 2013.

Boal, Augusto. *The Rainbow of Desire: The Boal Method of Theatre and Therapy.* London: Routledge, 1995. Print.

Bogart, Anne. *A Director Prepares: Seven Essays on Art and Theatre.* London: Routledge, 2001. Print.

---, and Tina Landau. *The Viewpoints Book: A Practical Guide to Viewpoints and Composition.* New York: Theatre Communications Group, 2005. Print.

Bois, Yve-Alain, and Rosalind E. Krauss. *Formless: A User's Guide.* New York: Zone, 1997. Print.

Bourriaud, Nicolas. *Relational Aesthetics.* [Dijon]: Leses Du Réel, 2002. Print.

Costello, Robert B., ed. "Walk." Def. 1. W*ebster's College Dictionary.* 3rd ed. New York: Random House, 1995. 1498. Print.

de Certeau, Michel. *The Practice of Everyday Life.* Berkeley: University of California, 1984. Print.

Hagen, Uta, and Haskel Frankel. *Respect for Acting.* New York: Macmillan, 1973. Print.

Hanh, Nhat. *A Guide to Walking Meditation.* Trans. Jenny Hoang and Anh Huong. Ed. Robert Aitken and Joseph Bobrow. Nyack, NY: Fellowship of Reconciliation, 1985. Print.

---. *Peace Is Every Step: The Path of Mindfulness in Everyday Life.* Ed. Arnold Kotler. New York, NY: Bantam, 1991. Print.

Khalsa, Gurucharan Singh, and Singh Khalsa Harbhajan. *Breathwalk: Breathing Your Way to a Revitalized Body, Mind, and Spirit.* New York: Broadway, 2000. Print.

Landau, Tina. "Source-Work, The Viewpoints and Composition: What Are They?" *Anne Bogart: Viewpoints.* Lyme: Smith and Kraus, 1995. 13-30. Print.

McCurdy, Carmissa. "Walking Meditation." *New Life Journal: Carolina Edition* 7.6 (2006): 3133. Health Source - Consumer Edition. Web. 31 Mar. 2013.

Padro, Josie. "Labyrinth Walking: A Journey of the Body, Mind, and Soul." *Alive: Canada's Natural Health & Wellness Magazine* 342 (2011): 97-101. Consumer Health Complete EBSCOhost. Web. 31 Mar. 2013.

Rosenberg, Elissa. "The Geography of Memory: Walking As Remembrance." *Hedgehog Review* 9.2 (2007): 54-67. Humanities International Complete. Web. 31 Mar. 2013.

Russell, Larry. "Learning to Walk." *International Review of Qualitative Inquiry* 1 (2008): 583-602.

Sexton, Shannon. "Meditation in Motion." *Yoga + Joyful Living* 110 (2010): 56. Consumer Health Complete - EBSCOhost. Web. 31 Mar. 2013.

---. "Walking Meditation." *Arthritis Today* 24.6 (2010): 36. *Consumer Health Complete EBSCOhost*. Web. 31 Mar. 2013.

Smith, Jean. *Breath Sweeps Mind: A First Guide to Meditation Practice*. New York: Riverhead, 1998. Print.

Solnit, Rebecca. *Wanderlust: A History of Walking*. New York: Viking, 2000. Print.

Spry, Tami. *Body, Paper, Stage: Writing and Performing Autoethnography*. Walnut Creek, CA: Left Coast, 2011. Print.

Sutton, John. "Memory." *The Stanford Encyclopedia of Philosophy*, Winter 2012. Web. 30 May 2013.

Vaughan, Laurene. "Walking the Line: Affectively Understanding and Communicating the Complexity of Place." *Cartographic Journal* 46.4 (2009): 316-322. *Academic Search Premier*. Web. 11 Feb. 2013.

Waxman, Lori. "A Few Steps in a Revolution of Everyday Life: Walking with the Surrealists, the Situationist International, and Fluxus." New York University, 2010. United States New York: *ProQuest Dissertations & Theses A&I*. Web. 11 Feb. 2013.

Wunderlich, Filipa Matos. "Walking and Rhythmicity: Sensing Urban Space." *Journal of Urban Design* 13.1 (2008): 125-139. *Academic Search Premier*. Web. 11 Feb. 2013.

## There's No Business Like Show Business! Teaching the Business of Acting

*Robert Woods*

 A college acting program is an insulated, protective, and creative environment in which the focus is on training students' minds and bodies, expanding their knowledge and understanding of the dramatic arts, and pushing the envelope of artistic expression so they can expand beyond their previous boundaries and limitations. In this artistic cocoon, it is easy to lose sight of the fact that show business is indeed a business, a business with both buyers and sellers. Actors are the sellers and their products are their acting services. Producers of stage, film, television, commercials, and web series are the buyers who are in business to generate profits. Actors are a necessary cog in that financial machine. The skills that actors need should not be limited to the dramatic; they also need business skills. They must learn how to market themselves, how to choose the right market for their services, how to pay their bills while they search for acting work, how to network and build their business contacts, and especially in today's technological world, how to produce their own projects. In any comprehensive actor training program, at least one course should address the business of acting. Such a course should be taught during the final year of study and should prepare acting students for the financial, contractual, legal, and emotional challenges they will face as true professionals in the world of Show Business.

 There are five broad topics that should be included in a Business of Acting course: self awareness, marketing tools and strategies, mentors, making a plan, and working practicalities.

### Self Awareness

 One of the most important lessons to be taught is how to identify an actor's own "type" or "brand." In college, young actors play all kinds of roles in many age ranges. I know of one young actor who put "Age range, 22 to 92" on his resume because he had also played old men in college. In the real world he will not be cast in those roles. He will find work only in his actual age range — perhaps 18-22 — and for his particular type. It is not a casting director's job to be imaginative about an actor's "potential." Producers want a casting director to bring in actors who can actually play the part. For stage productions, an actor's "type" may be somewhat more flexible, but for film, TV, and web series, an actor's "type" will be exactly what the producer, director, and casting director see when the actor walks into the room.

How can students be taught to identify their type? Several methods can be employed. The ideal method would be to bring in a casting director who can provide an expert opinion on how the students will likely be cast. Of course, casting directors may not be readily available in cities where little professional acting activity exists. This is where modern technology can be helpful. Casting directors can be brought into the classroom by Skype or other Internet video phone applications. This is not only efficient for the casting directors, but also saves the university the expense of paying for a guest speaker's travel. Why would casting directors participate? Because they are in the business of knowing actors. Casting directors are always looking for new talent, and where better to look than in college acting programs?

However, a casting director's analysis should not be the only informational source for students learning their type. One university program has its students choose five working actors who they believe are like their type, and the instructor then offers feedback, pointing out why the choices are accurate or not. Similarly, each student can pick five roles from professional productions (stage, film, or TV) that they believe they could play as well as the people who played them, and then be given feedback on those choices. In both exercises, an instructor must strive to keep personal opinions about the student out of the assessment. Because the instructor will have taught, cast, directed, and trained the student for several years prior to the business course, the instructor may not be entirely objective. The instructor will know a student's talents, abilities, limitations, and personality all too well. Even if the instructor remains reasonably objective, the advice given is just one person's opinion. Others may see the student's type differently.

Another college course has each student interview five random people on the street and ask them their opinion of the student's type. A variation of this would be to have the other students in the class weigh in on what they believe a student's type is. Employing several of these approaches will help students get an accurate reflection of their type, and they can then structure the marketing of their type to optimize their work opportunities.

Even with extensive input from the instructor, casting director, other students, and third parties, students may still not fully comprehend their own type. As all teachers have experienced, students do not always really hear what they are being taught. In preparing this paper, I interviewed a number of recent graduates from university drama programs (graduating between 2010 and 2015) who had taken a Business of Acting course. One of those, now pursuing his acting career in Los Angeles, said it took him years to really understand his type; what he learned in the business course was supplemented, or supplanted, by feedback from jobs he had booked and the roles his agent had sent him out for. Another graduate said that the only information given in her course was the opinion of her instructor, and she felt that she had no genuine idea what her type was when she arrived in Los Angeles. She had to learn it "on the job." What we can glean from these students is that this is a tough lesson to impart. Thus, the more exercises, and the more approaches that can be employed to help students learn their own type, the better the results are likely to be.

## Marketing Tools and Strategies

Once students have had a chance to identify their types, the next part of a Business of Acting course should focus on putting together marketing tools: headshots, business cards, a video reel, and a website. These tools need to be in the students' hands when they complete the class and certainly before they graduate and head out into the commercial world.

The first and most important tool is the actor's headshot. Headshots must look professional, be in color, and actually look like the actor. A headshot is not about looking "glamorous" or "dramatic" — it's about representing the actor's "type." Students in a business class should learn that there is no substitute for a professional headshot. It must be in sharp focus, especially the eyes, and the actor should be looking directly at the camera. The lighting must be good, with no strong shadows. This is a headshot, not film noir. The shot should generally be from the chest up, although full body shots can also be useful if the actor is seeking modeling work. Ideally, the student will work with a professional headshot photographer. One university program brings in professional photographers from Los Angeles or New York for a one or two day shooting session. This is good business for the photographers as they can shoot many actors in a brief time, and it is a good opportunity for student actors to work with pros and get headshots they can actually use in the commercial world. But if professional headshot photographers are not available in a particular college's area, or the budget is not sufficient to bring them in, professional portrait or wedding photographers may also work well. Students will surely have to pay for these headshots, but the investment is necessary as the headshot is the most commonly used marketing tool for any actor.

On the reverse side of the headshot photograph (printed on the reverse side or a separate sheet stapled on the back) will be the actor's resume. Students need to be taught how to format their resumes in a clean, easy-to-read format that can be scanned quickly at the audition to give a quick sense of the actor. The name must be at the top, and a good format also lists union affiliations under the name, height and weight off to one side, and representation (agent or manager) off to the other side. Credits should be broken into type (film, stage, etc.), with character names for plays or type of role for film and TV (i.e., lead, featured, guest star), and if the director or production company is well known, that should be listed as well. If the actor happens to have few credits, that is all right. The actor should include college credits and list any skills that might lead to a job: juggling, singing, playing musical instruments, horseback riding, sports, etc. Degrees and awards should also be included on the resume. Examples can be found online (http://www.ace-your-audition.com/acting-resume-samples.html).

Next, students must put together a demo reel, which the instructor should review and critique. No longer is having a demo reel optional for an actor. It is mandatory! And there is no reason not to have one. Technology today offers multiple options for creating a video reel. Cell phone cameras are of such quality now that professional short videos have been created on them; most digital cameras have video capability; and high quality video cameras can either be borrowed from family or friends who have one, or rented for reasonable prices. The footage can then be edited with several different computer programs. A demo reel used to be a resume of actual work, but now its purpose is to show how an actor looks and sounds on camera and to reflect the actor's type. Reels used to run 4-7 minutes; now they are about a minute long. The best clips should be placed up front, because casting directors are busy and their attention spans are short.

If the actor has no video footage from an actual film (long or short) or television program or web series, the reel can still be created. However, students should be taught not to shoot scenes with low budget equipment or skills. These will not look professional and will not showcase the actor's talent. Instead, students should shoot (with proper equipment, lighting and sound, of course) something they do well—a monologue, a song, a dance, a bit of a stand-up routine—essentially, a screen test.

If the university has a film department, this may provide an excellent opportunity for collaboration. Film students can be recruited to shoot drama students' demo reels, giving the film students an opportunity to work with actors, and at the same time yielding more professional-quality results for the student actors. Drama students should also be encouraged to act in student films, which will not only benefit film students, but will provide actors with footage for their demo reel.

If the university lacks a film department, the instructor should consider shooting footage in the Business of Acting course. A large amount of time in many such classes in college programs—probably too much time, given the nature of real world auditions—seems to be spent on the rehearsing and practicing of monologues. While monologues are still useful and required for auditions for professional repertory and regional theatres, Shakespeare companies and the like, the lion's share of auditions for stage, and virtually all auditions for film and TV, will be conducted from sides (short scenes) and cold readings. Devoting days and days of class time to just monologue work is inefficient. That work should be combined with filming those monologues (and/or songs, dance routines, stand-up routines, etc.). This will yield valuable material for the student demo reels.

Students should be required to create a website. In today's world, every actor must have one. There are numerous Internet sites that a student can use for developing and hosting a website, such as GoDaddy.com, Wordpress.com, Wix.com, Squarespace.com, and Weebly.com, to name but a few. Students today have grown up with the Internet and are likely more familiar with these sites than their instructors. The content of an actor's website should include headshots (not just one but several—smiling for commercials, serious for dramatic work, playful for comedy), the demo reel, the actor's resume (or multiple resumes for film work, stage work, and musicals) and bio, union affiliations if any, and of course contact information—telephone number and email address—and if the actor has an agent or manager, contact information for them as well. Additional optional information might include reviews of the actor's work in plays or films, and perhaps a blog to give casting directors and other industry professionals a better sense of who the actor is and what the actor is currently doing.

Next comes the actor's business card, which should incorporate the actor's headshot. In addition to the headshot, the business card should include the actor's phone number, email address, website address, and union affiliations. The back of the card can have anything that will make the actor marketable, like good review quotes or special skills. As part of the course, students should be required to get business cards professionally printed. They should be instructed that this marketing tool is too important for "DIY" (do it yourself) treatment. Numerous sources on the Internet are available for inexpensive printing of business cards.

Why does an actor need a business card, students might ask? The one word answer is simple: networking. Students should be taught that nothing cements an actor in the memory of a casting director, producer, agent, manager, or other industry professional more than a sharp business card that features a terrific headshot, and nothing leads to work in the industry better than networking. Networking, or "working a room," is a skill that must be learned and practiced, and the business course is an ideal place for that. There are many books on networking techniques that instructors can use to teach this component of the course, and a simple Google search of "how to work a room" will bring up excellent articles, videos, and other resources on how to network in a social situation. In my experience, however, there are basically three key points. Have a list of "ice breakers"—opening questions or topics they can ask to initiate a conversation (examples: "What did you think of so-and-so's performance in such-and-such movie/play?" or "I heard a story today about _____ and that reminded me of my favorite play/poem/line of dialogue . . ." or even just "What do you do in the business?"). Have a 30-second, interesting, funny story at your fingertips, ready to tell either in response to a question or as a networking conversational tool. And don't get trapped talking to one person the entire time. Make it a point to talk to at least five people for about five minutes each, and keep moving. Be sure to give each person a business card as you exit that conversation and ask for that person's business card in exchange. Once these techniques are taught, the Business of Acting course should provide networking practice opportunities, ideally with industry professionals, but if those are not available, then at least with guests who are strangers to the students and who are brought in to play the roles of industry professionals. Practice will mitigate the fear. As one recent graduate said, "People working in the industry are just people. Treat them like people, and you will lose your fear."

Another potential networking opportunity is available at the stage door. Any actor who is moving to New York, or Chicago, or even Los Angeles, should start off by seeing as many shows currently running as possible. When the actor finds a part he or she is right for, drop off a picture and resume at the stage door with the stage manager. Not only is this more personal than mailing a copy, it may open up the possibility of a chat.

## Cultivate Mentors

At the end of the musical *Gypsy*, the character Mama Rose tells Louise, who has become the star known as Gypsy Rose Lee, "No kid does it all on his own." And that is surely the truth. Every young actor needs to find and cultivate mentors, and a Business of Acting course needs to teach that, as well as teach ways to identify and establish mentors. Each student should have a 15-second "elevator pitch" to use as an introduction to a potential mentor: who the actor is, what the actor does, and the specific advice the actor would like to receive. One successful actress I know, who started her career as a ballet dancer, saw a Broadway star actor at a party. She approached him and used her elevator pitch: "Hi, I'm [her name], I'm a member of the [current ballet company], but I want to do Broadway. I'm a very good dancer, an okay singer, and I've been studying acting for two years. Can you tell me how you go about getting jobs on Broadway?" The star actor was impressed enough to introduce her to the dance captain of his show, who gave her practical information and invited her to a Broadway audition where he was assisting a star choreographer. He told her she wouldn't get the job because she was too young and too small, but he wanted to see her dance. At the end of the audition, the choreographer told her, "Keep auditioning. You belong in this business." Her elevator pitch to the star actor didn't get her a job, but it did give her practical information, including her type—young and small—and an introduction to a dance captain and a star choreographer. Shortly afterward, she took the dance captain's advice to audition for everything so people would get to know her. She auditioned for the Vietnam tour of *Hello, Dolly!*, and, at the end of the audition, she was offered a job in the Broadway production. The company needed a replacement (young and small) for one of the twins. Two weeks later she made her Broadway debut.

Mentors may be found everywhere and they come in all types: successful actors, directors, casting directors, producers, choreographers, agents, and managers. They can be found at industry events, such as screenings and film festivals and parties, or met at auditions, or even found in acting classes, dance classes, and workshops. Prior graduates of the university's drama school are natural choices for mentors. Every school should have a list of graduates and where they are working, and provide that list to new graduates. The class should also instruct students how, and how not, to approach a mentor. Do have the elevator pitch ready and present it nicely, cheerfully, and with a smile. However, don't interrupt someone's dinner or attendance at a show.

The Business of Acting class should not only discuss the importance of mentors, but also how to nurture the relationships and express appreciation. I knew a young actor who moved to Los Angeles. He was talented, tall, and good looking. I set up an appointment for him to meet with a casting director. Much to my surprise, he said he couldn't go. He had promised to attend an acting class with a friend, and so he felt he could not break that promise. This was a wasted opportunity because of poor prioritizing. The young man should have informed his friend of his chance to meet the casting director and arranged to attend the next acting class. Instead, he rejected my work in setting up the meeting, not only missing a golden chance, but leaving me to make excuses with the casting director. Another time, an agent I knew in New York agreed to represent a young actor on my recommendation. Before long, the agent arranged an audition for the actor for a small part on a network TV series. The actor did not get that part, but was called back to audition for a part in another episode. He didn't get that one either, but was called in for yet a third episode, which again he didn't get. The actor should have recognized that being called in time and again meant that he was liked and the show's casting director was just trying to find the right role for him, but instead he decided the agent was not helping him and stopped returning the agent's calls. Once again, my work as a mentor was wasted. Students should be taught that they cannot burn bridges in this business. It seems like a huge industry, but in fact it is quite small and word gets around. Mentors do not grow on trees. Students should be taught to cultivate their mentors and appreciate them.

## Make a Plan

Choosing the right city, or market, in which to launch a career is an important element of the class. A larger market will have more work available, but also a larger talent pool to compete against. A smaller market may be easier for a young actor to break into, to build relationships and get jobs. Los Angeles is known more for film and TV, but also has a thriving theatre business. New York is often thought of as being better for stage, and especially for musical theatre performers, but it also has a busy film and TV side. New markets open up all the time. Chicago and Seattle are great places for theatre; Dallas and Houston both have great theatre and also some film work; and Atlanta is a new hotbed of film and TV activity. A student needs to consider not only what type of work to seek and where his or her strengths will lead to work, but also what city will feel comfortable and "right" for that student to live in. If the environment feels uncomfortable, the actor will be miserable there. I have known young actors who tried out a city for a few weeks and then left, not because their talent wasn't up to the challenge, but because they just didn't mesh with the culture there.

A possible exercise in a Business of Acting class would be to have the students prepare a presentation for the class on their choice of city, justifying it by type of work desired, relative cost of living, people in the business they know in the city (including former graduates of the school they can connect with), people they might be able to stay with while they get on their feet (including relatives or friends of friends), and why the "feel" of the city is right for them.

One young actor who graduated in 2012 intended to go to Los Angeles, but instead followed his girlfriend to Hawaii. That small market turned out to be a boon. He was able to form a relationship with a local casting director and learned that TV shows and commercials filming in Hawaii want to book local talent if they can, to save money. During the next year, he booked some commercials and a sizeable guest star role on a network series, all of which provided good footage for his demo reel. When he did move to Los Angeles, he was already a member of SAG-AFTRA and had good credits on his resume. This is an excellent example of how a small market can work to a young actor's advantage.

The exercise of choosing a city should include a budget for that city. Students will have to research costs of apartments; cost of food (both cooking in and dining out); public transportation versus a car and the related costs for each (in New York, a car is a liability, but in Los Angeles, it is a necessity); costs of maintaining skills and appearance, including acting, singing, and dance classes, gym memberships, and even haircuts; costs of marketing, such as registration fees for casting websites, submission websites, a picture listing on IMDB (Internet Movie Data Base), as well as duplication of headshots, and paying for a domain name or website host; and even the costs of things that most students' parents had covered for them while in college, such as cell phone bills and health insurance. I surveyed recent graduates and found that, prior to doing such an exercise for their acting business class, most students had never prepared a budget at all. Their financial needs had always been taken care of by their parents. The research and preparation of the budget was an eye opener for many students, especially because their universities were located in towns with much lower costs of living than major cities such as New York, Los Angeles, and Chicago, or even Atlanta, Dallas, and Seattle.

The budget should include a pre-launch plan for saving enough money for moving expenses and getting established in a city prior to finding a day job. Although it sounds like a huge sum for a college student, $10,000 is really the minimum amount that should be saved before moving to a major market. This may require students to take a regular job in their hometown for a year or so after graduation and save, save, save before launching their career, but it is essential. For example, the average cost of a one bedroom apartment in Los Angeles ranges from $1,500 - $2,000 per month, so putting down the first month's rent, last month's rent, and security deposit means spending $4,500 - $6,000 immediately out of that saved $10,000.

The research done on the launch city may even help a student rethink his or her goals. I spoke with a recent graduate who was torn between pursuing acting in Chicago or teaching. She spent a summer there, but the city did not "fit" her. She reviewed the market research done for her Business of Acting class and realized it would be easy for her to rework the plan for becoming a teacher. She is now teaching high school theatre in her hometown and enjoying her work. This is an important lesson to be taught in any Business of Acting class. Not all graduates try to become professional actors. There are many other facets of this business, such as teaching, which are equally valid, valuable, and satisfying.

In teaching the above aspect of the business class, the instructor should pay special attention to current costs of living in the cities under discussion, and the instructor should attempt to determine which neighborhoods will most likely be chosen by young actors living in those cities. A survey of former students currently living in those cities will be helpful, as well as Internet research. A careful examination of each student's budget will also be important in making the exercise as useful as possible. It may also be illuminating for the students if recent graduates can be brought in, or Skyped in, to talk to the class about actual costs of living and surviving in their cities, and this of course will also aid in keeping the information up-to-date.

The budget exercise could also include a session on income taxes and the deductions available to actors. One university program actually conducts a tax and finances seminar and brings in a certified public accountant to talk about how to organize receipts and tax deductions. But this is probably not a useful component for the class for three reasons. First, most actors should not take on the responsibility of preparing their own tax returns. It is not what they are trained to do, and the risk of an expensive audit is too great. Tax return preparation is a job for professionals. Second, lists of the tax deductions available to actors is readily available from industry sources, such as the Actors Equity website, and both Equity and SAG-AFTRA also provide the Volunteer Income Tax Assistance (VITA) program to members. VITA provides free income tax preparation to low and moderate income entertainment industry individuals and their families. Third, tax returns and deductions are simply too esoteric a subject for college students to grasp. Most of them never have filed a tax return before—they are probably included as dependents on their parents' returns—so they have no real-life experience to relate to regarding this subject. If the subject of taxes is to be discussed at all in the class, it should be brief and for the purpose of raising awareness of available resources.

## Working Practicalities

There are three components of a working practicalities topic: performers' unions, actors' contracts, and the business and legal issues of producing projects. The first of these absolutely must be included in the business class. The rest should be included if there is time available and depending on the availability of expert guest speakers.

## Unions

Nothing says this is a business more clearly than the subject of the performers' unions, which include Actors Equity and SAG-AFTRA. Here, there are two issues that need to be included in the Business of Acting class: (1) the pros and cons of joining, and if joining, when to do so, and (2) how to become eligible to join the union(s).

Joining either Actors Equity or SAG-AFTRA is a capital investment. The initiation fee for Equity is currently $1,100, and the initiation fee for SAG-AFTRA is currently $3,000. Union membership pays off in higher compensation and greater protection from abusive working conditions, but for an actor just getting established, it may be unnecessary or even detrimental, because once an actor joins the union, the actor is prohibited from working any non-union jobs. In smaller markets, most of the jobs may be non-union, and even in large markets like New York and Los Angeles, there are many non-union opportunities that an actor just starting out may want to take advantage of, including many non-union commercials, which can be an excellent source of income and provide good footage for a demo reel.

This situation changes in "right-to-work" states, of course, because in those states all jobs are open to both union and non-union actors. Exactly half of the states are right-to-work states; Alabama, Arizona, Arkansas, Kansas, Florida, Georgia, Idaho, Indiana, Iowa, Louisiana, Michigan, Mississippi, Nebraska, Nevada, North Carolina, North Dakota, Oklahoma, South Carolina, South Dakota, Tennessee, Texas, Utah, Virginia, Wisconsin, and Wyoming. Notably not included are New York, California, and Illinois. In the right-to-work states, it may behoove an actor to join the union when a chance arises, as it will not prevent work in that state, but will give the actor an advantage when the actor moves to a larger market such as New York or Los Angeles.

In the Business of Acting class, actors should learn the requirements for joining the unions that cover the work they will be seeking. Current information can be obtained from the unions' websites. Another source of information can be guest speakers, brought in live or via Skype, who will provide up-to-date information and practices about union eligibility and the pros and cons of joining.

The Actors Equity website contains a page on "How to Join," which lists three methods for becoming eligible: (1) obtaining employment under an Equity contract, (2) being a member of a sister union for one year and working under that union's jurisdiction as a principal, or "under-five" contract (TV shows where the actor has less than five lines of dialogue), or at least three days of extra ("background") work, and (3) working in the Equity Membership Candidate Program at a participating theatre.

What this basic information does not reveal is the relative ease or difficulty of meeting any of those three eligibility criteria. Naturally, the most direct route is simply to attend the open auditions given for a union job and get the part. This can be done in large markets or small, but of course in a large market there will be more actors contending for that job. There are dozens of Equity theatres around the country. A list can easily be obtained by a Google search. The course could teach that when a young actor is ready to join the union, temporary relocation to one of these smaller markets might be a good strategy.

There are four methods of joining SAG-AFTRA. Those methods are not clearly explained on the union's own website. Unfortunately, in my experience SAG-AFTRA is a less non-member friendly union than Equity. Fortunately, information on how to join is readily available from other industry sources, such as Backstage.com.

The first method is to get a "Taft-Hartley" certificate. This is a term often heard by actors, but not well understood. The federal Taft-Hartley Act was enacted in 1948, affecting union jobs. For SAG-AFTRA, it allows a producer to hire a non-union actor when the producer cannot find an "available union actor" who possesses the "quality or skill essential to the role." Once the non-union actor is cast, the producer fills out the Taft-Hartley paperwork, and the actor is then eligible to join SAG-AFTRA. The actor can work for up to thirty days without joining, but for any work beyond that point the actor becomes a "must-join," meaning that the actor has no choice but to join the union in order to do the work.

The second method is to earn three vouchers while working as "extras" or "background" on a union film or TV show. This may not be that easy. Giving a voucher is at the discretion of the project's assistant director, and normally those background roles will go to actors who are already members of the union.

The third method is to be a member of a sister union for one year and work under that union's jurisdiction in a principal role.

The fourth method is relatively new and is acknowledged by many young actors to be an excellent way in. That method is to work in a SAG-AFTRA New Media Project. "New Media" is defined by SAG-AFTRA's website as "dramatic (scripted) and non-dramatic (non-scripted) entertainment productions intended for initial exhibition on a new media platform" (i.e. on the Internet, or accessible on a mobile device). This includes web series and videos. In today's tech-friendly world, a web series can be produced fairly easily and inexpensively. Even if it has only one episode, all principal performers will become SAG-AFTRA eligible. There is one hitch: there must be at least one SAG-AFTRA member on board the production, but that usually does not prove to be a stumbling block. The New Media project's producers can simply cast one union actor and then cast all other roles with non-union actors. All the non-union actors will earn a Taft-Hartley certificate. Several of the recent graduates surveyed became SAG-AFTRA eligible this way. One searched Craigslist for acting roles, found a producer doing a web series looking for actors, and joined up with him for the one episode they produced, and all the actors became eligible through self-producing that series. Another produced his own web series after he moved to Los Angeles and thereby obtained union eligibility. A third acted in a multi-episode web series produced by her friends in their college town, and so became SAG-AFTRA eligible before moving to her major market city.

## Actor Contracts

As an entertainment lawyer, I have been consulted far too many times by actors who worked without a contract, usually with "friends," and found themselves taken advantage of when it came to getting paid, getting copies of the video footage, or even getting reimbursed for out-of-pocket expenses. The worst cases involve actors who believed they were creating a film or video project together with their friends, only to be cut out of the editing or distribution or profits when their "friend" took over full control. All of this can be avoided if students are taught the oft-repeated, but frequently ignored maxim that "friendship is friendship, but business is business." Get a contract—always—and get it in writing. Oral contracts are legally enforceable, but it may be difficult to prove what the deal was. As movie mogul Samuel Goldwyn famously said, "An oral contract isn't worth the paper it's written on."

Actor contracts can be quite simple and entirely standard in their terms. SAG-AFTRA has simple form contracts on its website, and Actors Equity has a document library with rulebooks for various regional theatres. Sample actor contracts are readily available on the Internet via Google search. When an actor is offered a union job, the employer will offer the applicable union contract. The extent to which a contract can be negotiated depends on the flexibility of the employer offering it and the clout of the actor. Actors should be taught to read even form contracts thoroughly before signing them. This is not the place to sign first and ask questions later. All the terms of the contract are binding on the actor, whether the actor has read them or not.

A contract can also be written up by the actor and presented to anyone who offers that actor a job. All it needs to contain are the "five W's"—who, what, when, where, why. Who are the parties? What is the job? When and where will the job take place? And why is the actor doing the job, i.e., will the actor be paid and if so how much, or is the actor doing it for credit, a copy of the footage for the actor's demo reel, or other consideration? Write it up on paper, exchange emails or text messages, or even fax one (does anyone still use a fax machine?). All of those methods will work. Oh, be sure to get it signed!

Actor contracts can be considerably more detailed, of course. The contract I typically wrote for film projects ran eleven pages long and covered not only basic pay, but also participation in any profits made by the movie, placement of the actor's credit on screen in relation to credit for other actors, the actor's obligation to participate in publicity, and even such items as the type and contents of the actor's "trailer" or "dressing room." Stage contracts may include such terms as an actor's right to be part of the cast of a larger production (say, if the show moves to a larger theatre or a bigger city or goes on tour), billing, reimbursement for the actor's own clothes as costumes, and of course amount of base compensation and participation in any profits. I had one young actor consult me about the downside of not having a written contract. He performed in a workshop of a new musical. The producers "promised" the actors they would be part of the show if it went to Broadway, but didn't put that in writing. Sure enough, the show transferred to Broadway and became a hit—but the producers recast, and the young actor consulting me was not included. These stories are far too common, which is why students must be taught to get that contract in writing.

College acting professors are not lawyers, of course, but this would be an excellent opportunity to bring in an entertainment lawyer as a guest speaker. Entertainment lawyers in Los Angeles or New York can speak to students via Skype, and they are usually happy to donate an hour of their time because they can expect that some of those students will end up in their city and will need a lawyer when they begin getting work, so talking to the students is a good business development tool for the lawyer.

*Business and Legal Issues Involved in Producing*

It is tough for new, young actors to become known, especially in a large market. More and more, actors are also putting on producer hats, creating their own projects to put themselves out there and get exposure. Technology has made this easier and vastly less expensive than it used to be. This development means that a Business of Acting course needs to address the business and legal issues that arise in connection with producing, whether for stage, film, video, or Internet. Those business issues generally break down into two broad categories: contracts and copyrights; here again, an entertainment lawyer as a guest speaker can be very useful.

Whether producing for stage or camera, a producer must have a written contract with each person working on the project. That includes actors, crew people, theatres (if renting), locations (if filming in privately owned space), and of course playwrights and screenwriters. Not having a contract can easily lead to disputes and confusion. Most of those contracts can be quite simple, one page documents. Templates for these contracts are available from many industry books or can be found on the Internet, and these can be provided as handouts in the Business of Acting class. Volunteer Lawyers For the Arts is an excellent source for actors as are the many sites offering "free templates for business contracts."

With respect to the issue of copyright, students need to be taught that any existing work (play, screenplay, book, or other material) is still under copyright protection if it was written after 1921. Works prior to that date are generally in the public domain, meaning they can be used freely, although there are exceptions to this rule, and it may be wise to consult an entertainment lawyer. No copyright protected work can be produced—whether for profit or not—without a license from the copyright owner. Most stage plays can be licensed from Samuel French, or Dramatists Play Services, Inc., or for musicals, Music Theatre International. However, many works are controlled by their authors. For example, all Rodgers & Hammerstein musicals are controlled by the Rodgers & Hammerstein Organization (www.rnh.com). It may be necessary to do a little research to track down the rights for a play, but producers are legally required to do so. New plays that have not previously been produced must also be licensed by contract with the playwright. The last thing any producer wants is to face a copyright infringement lawsuit on opening night.

What if the producer is creating an original work, such as a film, a web series, or an original play? Unless the producer is also the writer, there must be a contract with the writer, granting the producer the right to produce that work. If the producer is commissioning a screenplay or any written work to be produced for film, TV, video, or Internet, the contract must be written, must be signed by the writer, and must contain a work for hire clause. Under the U.S. Copyright Law, when a work is "made for hire," the employer or other person for whom the work was prepared (including a producer) is considered the author and is the owner of the copyright in that work. Note: this rule does not apply to stage plays. The Copyright Law does not allow a play to be commissioned as a "work made for hire." While a theatre or producer may indeed commission a playwright to write a new play, the copyright in that new play will belong to the playwright, not to the producer or theatre. The only way for the producer or theatre to acquire ownership of that play is to buy the copyright from the playwright by appropriate written contract.

Students should also learn that, when they create an original work, whether as producer or as writer (or both), they should register the copyright with the U.S. Copyright Office. This is not expensive, and all information and forms are readily available on the U.S. Copyright Office website (www.copyright.gov).

### Structuring a "Business of Acting" Course: A Summary

To summarize, a Business of Acting course should teach students to understand their own type and age range. It should teach them marketing skills, and by the end of the course they should have headshots, resumes, business cards, and a website. They should have a plan of action—a target city, a budget, and a plan for support and/or a financial cushion. They should know the importance of mentors: how to find them, cultivate them, and respect them. And it should teach the working practicalities of being a professional actor—the pros and cons of and requirements for joining unions, the importance of always having a written contract, and an understanding of the business and legal issues involved in producing their own projects or creating new works.

When a business course is added to the acting curriculum, students can graduate equipped not only with polished acting skills, but also with marketing and business skills. In this way, they will be much better prepared to tackle the Business of Show Business.

*Photo by Ellise G. Lesser*

## An Interview With Zoe Caldwell:
## Part of the Master Series at the Pace School of the Performing Arts, Schimmel Center for the Arts, New York City

*Cosmin Chivu*

**Zoe Caldwell:** This filled up so quickly, when I went backstage there were three people. I thought, 'That's a tiny audience, but I bet they're great;' and I come back and there are a million. There are people outside begging to get in.

**Cosmin:** Welcome to Pace University. We are delighted, honored, and would like to give you a warm round of applause for accepting to be here tonight.

**Zoe:** Thank you.

**Cosmin:** I am actually going to start right away and I am going to ask you something about this picture right here. Who is in that picture and where?

**Zoe:** Well, she is a funny little Australian girl of seven, who because they lived in a sort of slum, and poliomyelitis was big time, I was sent to the Seventh Day Adventist school and that's the outfit I had to wear everyday; gloves and all. And when someone rang me from W. W. Norton, to ask me would I write a—what is it called? Memoir. A memoir?

**Cosmin:** Yes.

**Zoe:** I said, 'Thank you so much,' but truthfully, I don't write anything. Even letters. And he said, 'Oh, Ms. Caldwell, we don't want to know everything, we don't want all your successes and all your lovers.' I thought, 'What else is there?' He said, 'We just want you to start at the beginning of your life, try to remember everything both as a woman and as an actress. And when you get to the part where you feel you are formed, both as a woman and as an actress,

*Published by W.W. Norton, 2002*

stop.' So I sat down and I said, 'I am born, who am I, blah blah blah.' This was just a little while ago mind you; this isn't the little girl writing her memoir. When I finished it I gave it to him and he said, 'You've done it too quickly.' I said, 'No one told me it was supposed to take a long time.' And he said, 'Oh. Well, you have any idea what you'd like to call it?' I said, 'Yes I do. I want to call it 'I will be Cleopatra.' He said, 'I think that is a little grand.' I said, 'Aha. I have a photograph of myself on the way to school when I was seven, and if you have the courage to put it on the cover, all grandeur will disappear.' That is the reason that picture is on the cover.

**Cosmin:** Was that suitcase full of books or…?

**Zoe:** No. It was just for the foods I couldn't eat as a Seventh Day Adventist. It was a lot of meat and stuff like that—I sat alone at the end of the lobby and ate at lunchtime.

**Cosmin:** Around 1958/1959 you left Australia for London, and one of the first productions you were in was *Othello* and you played Bianca. Tell us about the challenge, after a lot of experience in Australia, the challenge to perform for a British audience and how is that different than an Australian audience.

**Zoe:** No difference. Our job is to pass on what the playwright has written. We're workers in the vineyard. We are not artists. The writer is the artist. So it is the same way everywhere, in whatever country, the same demands should be made of you. Tell the story. Obey the writer.

**Cosmin:** Let's talk a little bit about Mr. Guthrie: when did you meet him? Where? And how was your first interaction with Tyrone Guthrie?

## Zoe Caldwell Interview

**Zoe:** Well, the Royal Shakespeare Company. It wasn't royal when I was there. They always had the understudies go to wardrobe to be measured for a costume should they be asked to play. Then they asked the five directors, who would direct five plays for the next season, to be present at the performance of the five understudy plays so they know what they have to work with. And I was told that Tyrone Guthrie — he wasn't a knight then, it was a pretty unroyal group — that he wanted me to play Helena in *All's Well That Ends Well*. I never read *All's Well That Ends Well*, but I said, 'How lovely. I am there. That's good.' And then we got on with life.

I went on tour for two months and when I came back, I was introduced to this extraordinary man, who said, 'You are Helena and I'm your director.' I mean that season, can you believe the second season I was there I played Helena directed by Tyrone Guthrie and I played Bianca in *Othello*, which was cool because I played opposite Albert Finney and that was good. And then they said, 'The next thing you will play is Cordelia, opposite Charles Laughton, directed by the head of Stratford.' But before *All's Well That Ends Well* started rehearsing I went to Denmark to stay with my old friend who had written a play, a very important play, and he kept offering books that I was going to play in. I told my friend and his wife, with whom I was staying, what I was doing and he said, 'If you're playing Helena, why are you always talking about Hamlet, Hamlet, Hamlet, Hamlet?' The reason I was talking about Hamlet so much is because we lived on the Strand Line, which, if you keep on going, gets you to the castle. You get to Elsinore and it is on a promenade that goes right out into the ocean. And I couldn't believe what a beautiful castle it was. I couldn't believe that in all the times I've seen Hamlet I never heard any seabirds. And if you are that cut off from the rest of the world, and jutted out into the ocean, what are you going to hear? Apart from 'To be or not to be?' You're going to hear seabirds. So I kept coming back every night and saying, 'Why aren't there any seabirds in *Hamlet*?' And my friend said, 'Look, you are not going to play Hamlet. You are going to play Helena in *All's Well that Ends Well* and you don't ever talk about Helena. Now, have dinner, go to bed, and I don't want to hear from you until you've read it three times.' So I went to bed. I had no idea it was such a big part. And I said, 'Ray! Ray! I've been reading it, I've been reading it and there are so many soliloqusies.' And he said, 'The word is soliloquy.' So I told that to Tyrone Guthrie when I first met him. I thought it would be a charming warming-up thing to tell him when I first met him. And ever since then he would say, 'Right Ms. Caldwell, one of your soliloqusies.' Marvelous man! A great pathfinder. And you just had to follow him.

**Cosmin:** And soon you became involved in the Stratford Shakespeare Festival. The press started to call you a Shakespearean actress. You did a lot of Shakespeare around that time. Most of the plays were directed by Guthrie. You came to Canada, you came to America, and eventually you ended up in Minneapolis. Tell us about that journey.

**Zoe:** Well, the reason I was in Minneapolis was because The Minneapolis Company was formed by Sir Tyrone Guthrie. He was a knight by then. And I had been away in Australia going to the Outback to find myself. I went with a marvelous Australian fella, and I thought if I could just go into the Australian Outback with an Australian man, I would know what being an Australian woman is. I'd never known what it is to be an Australian woman. I've always been wealthy, welcomed to great hotels, traveling aboard great ships, so I better find out.

While I was away, Tyrone Guthrie wrote a letter to my mum, and he said that he was going to open a theatre in Minneapolis called The Guthrie Theatre. And he wanted me to be in the company. And my mum wrote back, saying, 'Thank you for asking Zoe. She'd love to come cause she so likes Minneapolis.' I'd never been to America let alone Minneapolis. And he wrote back and said, 'That's great. Then can I have your word that she will arrive?' Mum said, 'Oh yes, oh yes, she'll love it there.' Well guess what? I didn't love it in Minneapolis, but I had the most marvelous time with a wonderful company—it's always pretty exciting in the beginning.

## Zoe Caldwell Interview

**Cosmin:** I want to go back to the Shakespeare festival to mention the production of *Antony and Cleopatra*, when you met and worked with Christopher Plummer. I want to know a little more about that. What was your first encounter with Christopher Plummer?

**Zoe:** With Christopher? I was already a part of the Stratford company in Canada and one day Michael Landon, who was the director of the company, said, 'I want to do a production of *Antony and Cleopatra* and I would like you to play Cleopatra and Christopher Plummer will play Antony.' I said, 'Fair enough.' And then I started to work. I worked a lot with a wonderful designer named Tanya Moiseiwitsch, and I knew she was going to do the costumes, so I said to Michael, 'Can I go with Tanya Moiseiwitsch to the Metropolitan Museum in New York? Because not only will I see all the great Egypt sets, but I will also see the marvelous Roman sets, because she was very much part of both. And I'll wait for Christopher.'

Christopher was in Paris doing—who's the man who makes love to his mother? A Greek man. Could be anybody today. And then he has no eyes. Who is it? Oedipus. He was doing a film of Oedipus. And I couldn't wait. And I couldn't wait. And I couldn't wait. And I couldn't wait. And I had to keep rehearsing with a dreadful—very butch—but dreadful actor. Christopher never arrived. And the company—you know what companies are like—the company kept saying 'It's terrible, it's disgusting the way he is treating you. He is allowing you to rehearse with that dreadful man and he's in Paris.' I said, 'Yes, but he's playing Oedipus.' And they said, 'No, it's not fair, not fair.' I thought it was perfectly fair. I've got the time to do all my homework, and boy when I do homework do I do homework! I had filled the little place that I had outside of Stratford with paintings and pictures: everything I could, all the fragrances. So then eventually they said Christopher was coming tomorrow and I thought, 'Come, I can face you.' You know the shape of the Stratford theatre. It's a lot like this theatre.

Well, I came on dressed in my rehearsal costume, and all the company was in their rehearsal clothes just waiting for Christopher. The doors flung open and there was Christopher. In white. All white. And he was very, very tan. He strode up onto the stage, took me in his arms, and kissed me. The company could say nothing anymore. We never were lovers. That's one thing about theatre. If you're really working well with an actor or an actress, I beg you, don't be lovers because that means you'll have secrets and you'll cut the audience out. Whereas if you love the person you're working with that's great but don't ever have secrets from the audience with the person you're working with. So I was lucky enough to be married to one of the best fellas in the world, a wonderful producer called Robert Whitehead and I was already living with Robert and Robert was Canadian and had grown up with Christopher Plummer, growing up beside him so they were like brothers and I've never in my life had a better experience with any actor.

**Cosmin:** And you directed Christopher Plummer later on.

**Zoe:** Yes, I directed him as Iago opposite James Earl Jones. (After a long pause) Christopher Plummer. He's 83 and looks 70. He's divine, just divine and I thought I can't stand up in front of all these people and say 'Christopher Plummer is the greatest actor to ever walk this blah blah blah.' I couldn't do that so I said I know what I'll do. I say 'Thank you so much and I'm so grateful to be here on an evening when you're showering such honors on my brother. On her 'brother' you ask. I didn't know Christopher Plummer was her brother. No, he's not my brother. It's just that I've known him for fifty years and I've directed him and he's directed me and I've played with him and he's played with me and I've cheered him and he's cheered with me and yet we've never been lovers and I figure he's got to be something special to me. 'He must be my brother' and everybody adored it. Well, that's the kind of easy group we were.

**Cosmin:** In 1966 you won your first Tony with a Broadway production of *Slapsticks Tragedy* by Tennessee Williams. It was your second

Broadway production obviously here in New York. It was probably a challenge to leave a company to be a part of a production built totally on individual actors.

**Zoe:** I had been in plays in London. I had been in plays that weren't part of a company but this was very special because I had come down to replace Anne Bancroft. I had come down from Minneapolis to take over for her. She was wanting three weeks off to go to the Bahamas and they asked would I come down and do it. I said sure but let me see the production. I looked at the production and it was dreadful. It was at the Broadway Theatre but it was the most dreadful production. Jason Robards played a marvelous priest except he couldn't do it because it's not in his nature to do it. It's in Christopher's nature but not Jason's.

I went to Alan Schneider, the gentleman who directed, and said, 'Hello its very nice to meet you and I'll come down and play the part but I'll play it properly and I'll want none of your help.' And he was so grateful to get away from it that he said, 'Fine you do it your way.' He said 'I want to introduce you to Tennessee Williams,' so I went to his apartment and Tennessee was smiling as he was always smiling like that and he didn't know what to say because I was so wrong, absolutely wrong for the part that they wanted me to play. I was supposed to be the gossip columnist who was attacked by big huge birds and I was also supposed to be high on marijuana all the time and I didn't even smoke or had ever smoked marijuana so that was some research I had to do and I thought okay, now what is it she needs? I've got to do pratfalls, three pratfalls when I come in, so I went to the circus and I asked if they had someone who taught pratfalls. Yes, they did, so I was taught, I was taught how to do pratfalls then I thought—I was supposed to wear white face. Clowns we were supposed to be and also I was supposed to have this strange accent but I had never been to Key West and then going up in the elevator to see some friends of mine a woman said 'feeyash' and I thought, what did she say, and she said 'fish,' but she gave it about five syllables and I thought that's how I'm going to speak, that's a wonderful, wonderful accent. I based my accent on that woman who was just going up in that elevator and then Alan started to give me the most terrible instructions.

I was the gossip columnist and a friend kept a house for rundowns and we sat there on the veranda smoking pot saying 'huff huff huff weeeee.' But Alan kept having us, Kate Reid, a brilliant actress, Kate Reid and myself in white face were supposed to, by Alan's instructions, run around the house whereas in the script Tennessee had us come in, sit down, and not move and just smoke occasionally. We rock slow in unison. It was fine. Occasionally we rocked out of unison and got on top of the chairs, but we never left the chairs. So eventually I went to Alan and I said 'Alan I admire you enormously and I'm very grateful for you getting me this job, but I can't do it because everything you're asking me to do is everything Tennessee has deliberately told me I mustn't do as a gossip columnist. So you've got three more weeks, I'm getting out, and I wish you great luck with the play' and left and Alan couldn't believe that I would do such a thing. Eventually he got on the phone and said, 'If you come back, I promise you I will not give you any instruction.' What a big man to do that and that's exactly what happened.

There was a young man there on a Fulbright and I said 'I have to have someone there who follows me in the text.' He said 'Alright, take this fellow.' So I said to the young man, 'If I say anything in the text that is not there, if I make a stop when it should have been a semi-colon, tell me tell me tell me because all we will be doing is following Tennessee's instructions' and that's what I did. That's all I did—followed Tennessee.

The play lasted three days and I got a Tony. Now I didn't get a Tony because I was so brilliant. I got a Tony because all my listening was done to Tennessee. I never met him really except in his apartment and I knew he only wrote first thing in the morning like 2 AM until 6 AM so I couldn't go knock on the door and say, 'I've got a couple

*Photo by Ellise G. Lesser*

of questions.' I didn't do that. I said, 'I've got it here. He's written it here. I don't need to see him, I just did what he said. I got a Tony. That's the first.

**Cosmin:** Second one. Second Tony was in 1968 with a Broadway production of the *Prime of Miss Brodie*, correct? And we're not going to spend a lot of time because I would love to ask you some questions related to the craft since we have acting, directing—

**Zoe:** We don't need any more. Let them ask.

**Cosmin:** Yes. Then, moving on. How long does it take you when you perform to get into the body, the skin of the character?

**Zoe:** From the moment I wake up. I'm not good fun for a husband or children or dogs because no matter how clever you are they know that you don't care—they know.

**Cosmin:** So you're waking up as Medea for a year while you're performing?

**Zoe:** Don't think I'm saying I woke up and (very loudly) ROAR!

**Cosmin:** No, that's not what I'm saying but when you brush your teeth, you know, shower —

**Zoe:** My whole day was for her and I did nothing that would get in the way of her. Then of course I get to—I'm a Virgo which is pretty boring—but I get to the theatre three hours before and I take everything out, everything that has any connection with me, and then gradually I put everything that is connected to her on my body, in my body, until eventually about 30 minutes before curtain and then I open my door and anybody in the company can come and talk and laugh and gossip.

**Cosmin:** Did you have any nights when that didn't happen?

**Zoe:** Of course.

**Cosmin:** And what did you do?

**Zoe:** Well, you pray. You pray and you work a bit harder. I tell you when I was playing I would go and stand at the side of the stage and hold my hands in the air and eventually say, 'Why do I do this?' And I ask, 'Is it some call to theatre gods?' and I'd say, 'No, I have fat red hands and if I do that before I go on then all the blood runs down and I've got white hands' and that's better for Medea. Isn't that marvelous?

**Cosmin:** You've done a lot of Shakespeare and for some reason lots of colleges, universities, companies, theatres around America and Canada start by approaching Shakespeare by interacting with each other with a British accent.

**Zoe:** With what?

**Cosmin:** A British accent.

**Zoe:** Why? Those actors don't have a hold on Shakespeare. In fact you know George III didn't do anybody any good. George III said he couldn't say bath, he said 'both' and he couldn't say path, he said 'poth' and everybody close to him said, 'It's the King's English so speak it.' So everyone starts saying it. That's what actors used to say. Your accents, your American accents are much closer to Shakespeare

*Photo by Ellise G. Lesser*

than for whom he was writing and it makes me so mad when they say those British accents are so marvelous with Shakespeare. Rubbish!

Everybody is marvelous with Shakespeare or not; the one thing you mustn't try to do is try to help him. He is one writer that I know who doesn't need our help so you don't have to dramatically say 'To be or not to be,' just simply say 'To be or not to be that is the question.' When you're young and you don't have to worry about being your Hamlet because your skin and your body and your mouths are doing the work and therefore whoever you are you will be your Hamlet or Gertrude so never help him, just obey him. One day we should have a class where you do it for me. It'll be good so there we go.

**Cosmin:** Great. I'd like to open it up to our students. I'm sure they have many questions for you and then I'm going to ask one or two more questions at the end. Okay great, so who wants to ask?

**Audience Member (AM):** When you started your acting career what was your biggest challenge?

**Zoe:** Well I'll tell you. I had what now is called a learning disability or dyslexia or any of those grand names and when we give them those grand names we leave them alone, which is ridiculous.

What you've got to say is, 'You're dyslexic. Now what can we put in its place? What are you good at? Whatever you're good at, let's work very hard on that.' Forget dyslexia. I wish we did that with all our children because everyone can do something. They can bake a pie, sweep a floor; they can do something better than everybody else and if we really encourage them—you see I couldn't spell letters, and I couldn't deal with numbers—I still don't deal with them. I couldn't sew but I noticed when I was quite young that I could keep people interested and awake and in their seats by telling other people's stories so I thought, 'Hell, that's what I can do.' I could dance, tap dance, and sing but none of it well enough but I could keep them in their seats and that's what I did. Very young too.

**Cosmin:** Next question?

**AM:** Hi. I'm Rebecca. You've had the opportunity to play some incredible women by some incredible authors. I wondered if you could talk about what you've learned from the prolific characters you played and how it has impacted your growth as a woman or artist or actor.

**Zoe:** Every time I play some extraordinary women or even some old woman, I learn from them. And that's why I realized I could do a memoir because I realized each time that I was little more formed, a little more formed but we can learn from anything, a train ride, a bus ride, seeing you just now walking down the aisle. God, I loved the way you walked down, marvelous body, and if you noticed what you've got to do is keep your eyes open. No texting. If you do that the whole world goes by—look look look for me to make contact with you—I have to look in your eyes, in your eyes.

I remember when walking the streets of New York was so terrific because you'd catch somebody's eye and you'd smile or you'd see a couple who were having a terrible fight and you could be involved in that. Now its terribly miserable walking the streets of New York. The only ones I talk to are ladies in a pram because they're sitting like this. Mum's texting, nanny's on the mobile phone. Nobody is talking to them and I bend down and I say 'Hello my beauty how are you?' and they connect. They need to connect, all of us need to connect with other humans. You can do it with dogs if you like, but human beings! Did I answer your question?

**AM:** I think so.

**Zoe:** If you're in any doubt ask me again. Think about it and ask me before I leave. No good after I've left.

**Cosmin:** Next question.

**AM:** How did you learn how to relax into your parts as a person, and as an actor?

**Zoe:** Well, I tell you I don't know that I'm so relaxed, but if I seem relaxed that's great. I was very nervous about today because today I've got this terrible cough. It's no good and I thought, 'I don't know them. How many of them will there be?' But I knew you were young and that thrilled me. That idea and the anticipation of being with you who are young was really exciting. I did nothing. You can see I didn't spend a lot of time on my hair but we went through the wrong door and the driver said we had to pay our way and it was so cold where we were standing and I thought, 'This is a load of rubbish that I'm coming to, I don't understand why am I so nervous?' Then I saw three people here and I thought, 'Three people. Wouldn't you know?' and then I suddenly came in with you holding my hand and all the faces faces … young young minds … eyes eyes eyes eyes.

**Cosmin:** Shawn is going to ask the next question.

**AM:** We focused a lot on your stage career but you also have a great film career as well so I was wondering—

**Zoe:** No, I don't! Sorry Shawn, I'm not a film actress, I don't have a film career.

**AM:** Oh, but you've done film.

**Zoe:** I'm rotten in them.

**AM:** I was wondering if you found a big difference in acting for stage and acting for the screen and if you have how did you overcome that?

**Zoe:** Did I what?

**AM:** If you found any difference in acting for stage or film.

**Zoe:** Oh, a world of difference. A world of difference, and I think you've got to love to be filmed. You know, the really great ones loved having a camera and they made love to the camera. I'm feeling, 'Get the camera out of the way, get the camera out of the way.' I'm not a film actress. I admire film work. I admire those who do it marvelously and there are so many who do it marvelously, but I'm not one of them.

**AM:** Thank you.

**Zoe:** But thank you, Shawn. Here she comes. Watch her walk. Hello.

**AM:** Hi, I'm Lindsay. You talked a lot about the process you have getting into a character. You dedicate so much time to that, so I was wondering how you get out of a character.

**Zoe:** Oh, you are bright. That's a marvelous question. Do you know it takes me sometimes six months to retrieve me and for me to be a proper wife, mother, and owner of dogs? But it can take that long. Also my body, whatever my body has become. Big, skinny skinny skinny. I thought Medea must be skinny skinny skinny because she's going through such terrors and Emma I knew was fat fat fat fat fat and it was up here so I couldn't have things stuffed, it had to be my arms were fat my neck was fat. Ian Holm was … who's the fella?

**Cosmin:** Lord Nelson.

**Zoe:** Oh yes. Nelson, Lord! Right. Lord Nelson yes, funny little chap. He used to travel around England and speak to various little gatherings of people in towns and he'd be there with his one arm and one leg and one eye and he'd suddenly say, 'Oh wait, wait we're missing a town; no, no we didn't do this town.' He wanted to be adored, isn't that marvelous? One would say, 'Lord Nelson, he wouldn't want to be adored' but he loved it, he loved it.

**AM:** Thank you!

**Cosmin:** Next!

**AM:** Hi, Ms. Caldwell, my name is Anthony.

*Photo by Ellise G. Lesser*

**Zoe:** Anthony?

**AM:** Yes.

**Zoe:** And I'm Cleopatra.

**AM:** I would love that—you mention a lot about your preparation and you always look at the text and you obey the playwright's punctuation, and it helps you get into your body. How about personalizing the text? How much of your own life do you take into the script?

**Zoe:** How much do I what?

**Cosmin:** Personalize.

**Zoe:** Personalize; perhaps you see that's my one bad thing. I don't think I personalize it too much. That's a problem. That's why it takes me six months to get back again, I am an observer when I am anywhere. I can never be bored if there's a human being hanging around because I watch them and watch them and watch them and watch then. Anthony, you're an actor?

**AM:** Yes, I am.

**Zoe:** Got a good voice in you. I can never be bored because there's always someone you can watch, when you are doing a part. It is amazing the way you suddenly find something, somebody in the crowd to watch, and you come home and you say, 'You know what was so extraordinary, bluh-bluh-bluh-bluh-bluh actually it is totally to do with the part I was playing and it would be totally different if it were a different part.' That doesn't answer your question at all.

**AM:** I think I understand where you're coming from.

**Zoe:** Ask me something else in that mode and get the answer.

**AM:** Right now? OK. When you're reading a script and you want to become the character, besides the punctuation, how much help would you substitute from your own life to up the stakes of the character?

**Zoe:** If I had to up the stakes to play the character, the writer is not a very good writer, because what is extraordinary and marvelous is if you just obey the writer and really get his message to you and you and you and you and you and you, that's very intimate stuff and it will, if everything goes well, provoke you—provoke you with something that's right for the play. If it provokes something that is wrong for the play . . . burn it! Go back to the writer. He'll help you.

I taught at Florida Atlantic University for about six years just in the summer—no, just after Christmas so I wasn't cold and I had a darling boy in my class who was, of course, gay. He was a sweet darling fella and one day he was doing something and he slapped himself in the face and I said, 'What did you do' and he said, 'Well its what I do to myself when I've done something wrong' and I said, 'Why would you do it to yourself,' he said, 'Well, I just do it.' So I got him onto 'to be or not to be' and I said, 'I don't want to hear anything but your voice, I don't want you to go in a deeper register because you are doing Shakespeare, I don't want you to do anything but use your own voice and I—I'm going to put my arm around your waist to give you support while you try this rather difficult task and as you get better and better at it I will remove the support I'm giving you and if you make a mistake, slap my face!' He never slapped my face, because he never made a mistake. And I found out later that the person who trained him to slap his own face was his father. So pretty nice huh?

**AM:** Thank you very much!

**AM:** Hi, I'm David.

**Zoe:** Oh how sweet, yes yes yes!

**AM:** So after a lifetime of working and playing on stage and around the world I want to know after looking back it at it, when did you feel like you got it right? How did you know?

**Zoe:** When I played Alice (Alice Hauptmann in *Elective Affinities* by David Adjmi) recently. I know that sounds silly and no one can believe it, but I suddenly said to Charlie, 'That is about as good as I'll ever be.' I am absolutely forceful, absolutely in character, absolutely Alice. And I guess its someone from on high and low, whatever—I am about to be seventy-nine, that means I'm almost 80 and I've had a wonderful career and life and I've just been made a grandma to twin boys. And I don't want to work, I want to teach cause that's the one thing I don't have to learn words for. To teach. But if I could do anything to help actors be as the actors of yesterday, I would do it that, that's what I would do.

**AM:** Thank you!

**Zoe:** David, thank you. Now we are going to have a lot of people come. Come on!

**AM:** I'm Molly. Nice to meet you.

**Zoe:** Molly? What a nice name.

**AM:** Thank you. My middle name is Esther so my mom called me Molly Esther—Polyester.

**Zoe:** Oh, congratulate your mom!

**AM:** I have a question; you said that when you prepared your role you work with fragrances, which is awesome because smell has to do with memory but every time I try it, it turns me off, like when I smell something and try to associate it with a part. So I was wondering how you do that. Like how do you pick a scent, how do you, you know, do research on a character?

**Zoe:** I have a different perfume for each character.

**AM:** That's what I'm saying—how do you associate? I want to try it. I want to do it. I've tried it but it doesn't work.

**Zoe:** Why doesn't it work?

**AM:** I don't know how to associate it, I'm sorry I don't know how to say it. I don't know how to associate the character I'm playing—I don't know where to start, where to go, 'Oh this character might smell like this, this character might smell like this.' Just recently in a show called *Fat Girls* one of my characters was an over-eater so I got a perfume that smelled way too sweet like candy. That would be ideal but it didn't work for me and I really want to make it work.

**Zoe:** Don't try.

**AM:** I don't know how and you make it work.

**Zoe:** Don't try. Just one day get into that character and one day you will pass a perfume bar or a woman in an elevator and you know that those two things go together. Don't work at it, let it come together, but you have to be open. And let it happen. When I was in *Othello*, the thing that I really adored about the play was Paul Robeson and he, I mean he was 65 or something and I was 24; we weren't in love and I adored him and he adored me and we would get into the corner and just laugh and the great thing about him walking down the halls was his beautiful robes, and the smell, it was one wonderful wonderful oriental perfume and people loved to walk behind him because he smelled so good and you'd say, 'What was your impression of Paul Robeson?' and they'd say, 'Oh he smells so good!' but don't try, dear Molly, just let it happen!

**AM:** Thank you!

**Zoe:** And Molly sweetheart, who is your character?

**AM:** I don't have any right now. I'm not working on anything.

**Zoe:** Oh well whoever your character is, might just come and say 'Molly, Molly, Molly smell this!' Okay?

**AM:** Thank you.

**Cosmin:** We have time for a couple more questions.

**Zoe:** Rum-tum-tum-tum-tum-tum-tum-tum! Yay! And who are you?

**AM:** Aiden.

**Zoe:** Aiden! That's an unusual name. Aiden?

**AM:** It's Irish.

**Zoe:** Oh yes, so strong, so strong. Now what are you going to ask me, Aiden?

**AM:** What was your first experience on stage like? Rehearsal and getting to know the play.

**Zoe:** I was in my first dancing concert at two years and ten months and I played with a little tiny ukulele and a grass skirt, "Lovely Hula Hands." That was my first appearance on the stage. But as I grew older, I watched other actors, I watched everybody and if somebody was needed to make a pot of tea I'd do anything for the theatre so nothing is held back, everyone is working, working, and gradually, gradually, gradually, you are getting more skills about what you need to know. What was your last part?

**AM:** Um…oh it was Fernando in *Fuente Ovejuna*.

**Zoe:** And how was that?

**AM:** It was unusual, 'cause I never played a character that had a happy ending before so that was good and it was nice to play the romantic lead.

**Zoe:** Oh, it is always good to play the romantic, just don't have the affair! Oh Aiden, what a great life you've got ahead of you but watch, watch, watch, listen, listen, listen, learn, learn, learn. It's all the regular stuff. You're obviously lucky to have good parents because that initial infatuation that your parents have with you as a baby, 'Look at him look at him look at him!' is what gives you strength and courage to go and do more and even more. I wish you great joy…

**AM:** In the development of actors there is always this controversy—

how much method to depend upon. How much do you depend on different schools? I'm just curious about your experience. What do you see are the pros and cons of adapting certain methods? I know the young lady, Molly, for example—that's something you often hear in schools about method acting. Pretend you are a Kleenex tissue or something and that kind of thing. I wonder if you had any thoughts about that.

**Zoe:** Oh, it's method acting you're asking me about.

**Cosmin:** What method do you embrace?

**Zoe:** Mine because it's the thing that makes me well. I will do anything for myself because that's my health. Does that make sense?

**AM:** Absolutely, you say you developed your own method essentially.

**Cosmin:** We have time for one more question.

**AM:** Hello Zoe, my name is Amanda. I'm just wondering—you've spoken a lot about the tremendous loyalty you have to exactly what the playwright has written and you talk highly about what physically a character is given, so I'm wondering, when you are rehearsing a role do you prefer to have large chunk of it memorized already and focus on the punctuation? Or do you sort of memorize it with your body? The body of the character?

**Zoe:** I memorize it with the body of the character, there is no good in having lines learned, you know. It isn't until you look up from that and make contact with your other actors that I can have a true humanity, but I think, I think I never, never, learn lines before—never.

**AM:** Thank you.

**Zoe:** You've got to know that what you're doing for a living is the thing that makes you well and strong. If you don't feel that, find something else. You've got to know this if somebody says to me, 'I don't know if I should get married or not' I say, 'No, don't get married, if you are going to ask me that question you shouldn't get married.' Same thing with 'Should I be an actress?' If you can ask me, then no. You want to kill to be an actress, you don't ask.

# Zoe Caldwell Interview

**AM:** Thank you.

**Cosmin:** You are currently working on your second book, would you like to say something about that?

**Zoe:** Currently writing! Right! Well, he said, 'I'll tell you what I want your second book to be.' I said, 'No, no, one book that's it, that's all I'm up to.' And he said, 'Think about this, when I read your first book, I was very clearly understanding Shakespeare because you were talking about it in a sort of colloquial way about what happened and you go through the characters and really know what it is about. I want you to start from the beginning when you were seven and absolutely every Shakespearean thing you have ever done.' He said, 'Put them all in a colloquial manner, what you learned from them and as you go further along the book, your demands of the play will be stronger than the ones at the beginning.' The first time I was asked to play Desdemona there was a huge white fella who was very rich in Melbourne and he asked me when I was 15, would I consider taking all the color out of my hair to play his Desdemona? And I said, 'Ah sure' which was because I didn't realize how obscene this production would be with him—great white fella and the things that he loved about doing Shakespeare was the costumes! So he had bags and bags and bags of sandals and jewels and cloaks and he never talked about the play, never, never, and I thought, 'How can I get through this?' In my book this is called, "The First Othello." How can I get through this, how am I going to get through this? I'll just pray, I'll pray that one day I will be in a company that tells the story. Many years later I was in the production in Stratford with Paul Robeson, Sam Wanamaker, Mary Ure, Albert Finney—is that not an answer to a maiden's prayer?

**Cosmin:** What's the name of the book?

**Zoe:** The book is *Shakespeare I Have Known*.

**Cosmin:** And when is the launching, how soon is it coming up?

**Zoe:** When is it coming up? Oh it's got to be written! I've written about five of my experiences, but you know when I got ill with this terrible thing, I just stopped writing, stopped doing anything. But now I'm becoming better again and I'll write again.

**Cosmin:** My last question is, if you were to give one piece of advice to a young actor, what would that be?

**Zoe:** Well, everything I've said is one piece of advice. I mean it's advice, advice, advice. You can't really give people too much advice about, about anything. About marriage, about . . . lovemaking, you've got to recognize and then give everything to whatever is needed. And when someone says, 'Ah, I've got an extra ticket to this marvelous concert' and an actor says, 'I can't go, I have a rehearsal. Because I have a rehearsal and I can't wait to go to rehearsal! I've loved being there.' That's an actor. So there we go.

**Cosmin:** I want to thank you.

*(Roar of audience applause)*

# The Actress Plays a Man:
## Making Neil Labute's *Reasons to be Pretty* Strange
### David Marcia

"The actress plays a man. PHILOSOPHER: If a man had been playing this man, he wouldn't have brought out his masculinity so forcibly, and seeing him—or the incident, to be more precise—played by a woman made us perceive as typically masculine many characteristics that we usually consider to be general human ones."
—Bertolt Brecht, *Brecht on Performance*

"Stanislavsky's sense (was) that the moment-to-moment performance of a role is the actor's present reality and truth. This paradox, which equates "truth" with 'theatricality,' opens the door to non-realistic aesthetics."
—Sharon Carnicki, *Stanislavski in Focus*

The production at the center of this article began by having nothing to do with this topic. It began, as most productions do, with the commitment to serve a good play and create an event worthy of an audience's attention. In the course of auditions, the production came under the influence of an idea that caused me to question how I had previously approached casting. What if women actors played the masculine roles (Schechner 26)? At first blush this was a radical but relatively simple notion. What if we treat a character's gender as simply one aspect of the given circumstances within the fictional world of the play and nothing more? Certainly, cross-gender casting has a long history in the theatre, but this history is all too frequently that of masculine or boy actors playing women characters because of societal prohibitions against the very existence of woman actors in the first place. The advent of so-called "breaches" productions were at least as much about the public exploitation of the woman actor's body as they were about artistic accomplishment and less about increasing the number of substantial women's roles in the classical repertory (Schechner 2010). Even Bertolt Brecht, whose quotation gives this essay part of its title and whose thoughts on this subject seem breathtakingly clear, never actually implemented them in production and neither did the Berliner Ensemble after his death (Barnett 113). Today, while the practice of women actors playing male characters seems to be increasingly accepted in Shakespeare, it is largely absent everywhere else.

As we applied this idea to *Reasons to be Pretty* and began to implement it in production, the actuality grew more complex, and as I now try to capture the experience in words, the implications are almost too vast to capture. How important is an actor's gender to their performance of a role? How might this apply to other actor/character attributes such as race, age, and physical type? What are the ethical pitfalls of any concept of "open casting" operating without regard for the societal effects of dominant power? Given the enormity and importance of these issues, I feel the best way to approach them is via the narrow route of a deceptively simple question applied to a single production. The production took place in 2011 at the University of Missouri and the question is: "What if women actors played the masculine roles?"

As I've said, the casting philosophy we eventually settled on was not a factor in pre-production. However, interestingly enough, the production team's decisions prior to auditions guided and supported the eventual casting. Specifically, we decided to shoot for the most minimalistic aesthetic possible in a full production. The space was the department's black box theatre in a converted Baptist Student Union. The stage configuration at the time placed the actors at floor level and the majority of the audience on staggered risers in front of them; the playing area jutted forward all the way to the first row of seats, creating somewhat the feeling of a thrust stage. While the stage area was fully draped, upstage entrances and exits could be problematic due to architectural limitations backstage. The audience entered through two wide aisles on each side of the house and we also used these for exits and entrances during performance. The set

# The Actress Plays a Man

consisted of a small square table and two chairs, used throughout the play and a small vanity table and bench for the first scene. A triangular cornice with its base facing downstage was also hung from the grid to unify the playing area. Lighting was focused in an "X" shaped pattern from up left to down right and up right to down left to facilitate and reinforce diagonal movement within and between scenes. Costume changes, for the most part, were to take place on stage in full view of the audience and the stage and costume crew were to be dressed in coveralls similar to those worn by the Greg and Kent characters when they were at work, but of different colors. The pre-show and transition music was to be early Elvis Costello, primarily from the "Get Happy!!" album, where the juxtaposition of jaunty pop melodies and bitter ironic lyrics commented on the previous scene and set up the following one. In total, the production plan was designed to highlight the actors and LaBute's language. Little to no effort was to be expended on hiding any of the theatrical machinery employed.

After auditions and call-backs, I was certain I had identified the four strongest actors who read best together. I had previously worked with all of them; three of the four had excelled in our department's training in Meisner technique and so possessed a common method and vocabulary. The only dilemma was that they were all women. If I proceeded traditionally, two of them would be uncast and two masculine actors of admirable, but demonstrably lesser ability would get those roles. I've directed plays for most of my adult life, professionally and in academia, and these are simply the breaks; we do the best we can with what we have. Or do we? Certainly my increasing immersion in performance philosophy was a significant influence, but to be honest, in the end, I was simply unwilling to consciously make the compromise I'd made unconsciously many times before. Given that we'd never discussed this casting option at any time in the audition process, I felt the only way to proceed was to do so. The four women were committed and enthusiastic, but at least at this point, their commitment and enthusiasm was for playing characters of their own gender. How might those positive emotions be affected by what I was proposing? Also, not insignificantly, the actors had been involved in two days of auditions and call-backs where they were in competition with each other. How might this affect their decision to sign on to a different casting philosophy? Fortunately, due to my preparation with the production team, I had some idea of what I thought our aesthetic should be. I was able to assure the yet to be cast that we would not be in the business of impersonating the masculine characters. We would discover how to create this aspect of their character as we would any other attribute, both organically, and in keeping with the actor's own sense of truth. We would not try to hide the actor's gender, nor would we attempt to accentuate it. After thirty minutes or so of conversation where the actors ended up talking more to each other than to me, all four agreed. The next potential stumbling block was who would play which character. Since all four had only read for Steph and Carly, we did another series of readings trying on nine or ten of the sixteen possible cast permutations. In the end, incredibly, we all pretty much agreed on who was best for each role, and I have to say it was the most satisfying night of casting I've ever participated in. To be able to move from a competitive audition environment to one of ensemble was remarkable, which is not to say that there was not a certain amount of backlash. A very few of the masculine actors objected to "their" roles being taken away; our dramaturg, who'd been part of and enthusiastically supported the casting, almost immediately reconsidered and sided with the disgruntled; the costume designer was livid over not being consulted. All in all, there was probably no more or less adversity generated than by a more traditionally cast production. Although, because of the unusual nature of the casting, some felt more justified in voicing their disapproval. A director's authority is a funny thing, perhaps most unassailable when it is most conventional.

In the course of rehearsal, we found that the most problematic scenes were generally the ones between Greg and Kent and that these scenes grew more difficult as the play progressed. For some reason, interactions between the different gendered characters, while always challenging, were generally clearer and more transparent to work on than scenes between the two masculine characters, leading me to the conclusion that sometimes masculine dialogue really is written differently. Communication styles vary on a continuum between genders, and good playwrights are adept at capturing these traits and nuances. This can frustrate actors and directors who aren't sufficiently attuned to these patterns of speech and behavior. While the different gendered scenes are hardly simple or straightforward, they are not generally as deeply duplicitous and manipulative as those between Greg and Kent (interestingly, there are no scenes between Steph and Carly). In these interactions, the circumstances LaBute creates seem to generate in the actors and audience the same conflicting drives and allegiances that define Greg and Kent's relationship and it can be both confusing and maddening to explore in rehearsal. Furthermore, I suspect this is the case regardless of the actor's gender. Words, phrases, and images are continually repeated, or more often, nearly repeated, with slight changes in wording at different times in a scene, making even accurate line memorization unusually difficult. One memorable evening, after working on scene four for over an hour, Tamara (the actor playing Greg) and Kristen (the actor playing Kent) grew increasingly frustrated with each other only to both simultaneously turn on our excellent and long suffering stage manager, Benjamin, for constantly interrupting them with slight line corrections (as we had agreed he would). Soon we were all sitting on the floor laughing nearly hysterically and it eventually occurred to me that somehow, LaBute had encoded all of both characters' bad karma into their language and we had, in a sense, overdosed on these negative emotions in rehearsal. What was revealed was that nothing was really as it appeared; what might at first seem like dialogue composed of near mindless repetition and a poverty of ideas, eventually revealed itself to be a carefully constructed and peculiarly masculine, passive-aggressive strategy for the extraction of information without giving anything in return, voyeuristic sexual satisfaction, and dominance. In order to explore this phenomenon in more detail, I will examine the progression of these scenes between Greg and Kent throughout the play.

Scene two (LaBute 11-14, 18-19) shows us the basic dynamics of Greg and Kent's friendship, which appears at first to be more or less a relationship of equals. They work the same night shift at the same warehouse, and Kent offers his attention, insights, and support in response to Greg's confused upset over Steph leaving him. However, as the scene progresses we see that both men have surreptitious motives. Greg is obsessed about Steph's conversations with Kent's wife Carly and wants either Carly or Kent to tell him what Steph has been doing since she walked out. Kent needs to keep the diffident Greg in line, both insofar as his play on the company softball team is concerned, as well as to cover for Kent as he considers pursuing an affair with another woman, Crystal. Kent controls Greg by using a classic bullying strategy. First, he interrupts and undermines Greg's break-up story by inferring he doesn't know the difference between a pot and a skillet, then Kent belittles and insults Greg for eating a power bar after his lunch and getting fat. Later at the end of the scene, once he's confident Greg is more or less beaten into submission, Kent appears straightforward, sympathetic, and supportive. These same dynamics become even more intense and obscure in the second part of scene four (LaBute 29-33) where neither Kent nor Greg is actually engaged in the conversation they appear to be having. Kent doesn't know if he can trust Greg, but he has to tell someone else—some other guy—in order to fully savor his affair with Crystal. In order to do this, he alternately ridicules, intimidates, and seemingly shares his wisdom about women with Greg, who initially only cares about weaseling out information about Steph, then realizes he's now responsible for the knowledge of Kent's infidelity. Kent's inner life is also revealed to be increasingly pornographic; it's not enough to cheat in secret—he has to obsess over the minute details and pull Greg deeper and deeper into it. Scene seven (LaBute 47-55) starts with Greg as diffident as ever, first hurt over Kent's avoidance of him, then guilty and wanting to extricate himself from the position of lying about Kent's whereabouts to Carly again in the future. This combination of defiance and betrayal brings out the very worst in Kent's increasingly unpleasant nature, driving him to violence and conversely, forcing Greg to at last stand up for something at least approaching what he would like to believe in. He doesn't just lose his temper and strike out, he beats the hell out of Kent in front of a crowd of co-workers because he thinks it's the right thing to do and the audience agrees with him. In general, the scenes between Greg and Kent seem to be especially well-served by actors concentrating on the circumstances of their relationship, informed by the contradictions of their behavior, rather than from an overly psychological approach, which the text seems to resist.

Physically speaking, our experience was that it simply doesn't take all that much to convey gender in performance. While everyone has their own experience of those qualities that convey masculinity and femininity, one or two key traits seem to serve the actor best, especially if the production doesn't go to any great lengths to hide or emphasize whether the actor is masculine or feminine. While gender is a complex cultural function, on stage it operates largely in response to certain specific attitudes and gestures denoting and connoting femininity or masculinity. We were supremely fortunate to have professional fight choreographer and stage action director Rick Sordelet in residence with us during the first week of rehearsal. The subtlety, depth, and brilliance of Rick's work is a subject for another article; in this one I must perforce focus on only one of the many insights he contributed to this production, namely, the profound difference a lowering of the actor's center of gravity can make in the portrayal of a masculine character. Figure one shows Kristen Walker (playing Kent), with this adjustment in place.

Figure two shows Tamara Mullins (playing Greg), with the adjustment in place and Kristen without it. Note the curve of her downstage leg and how it extends upward and out through her upstage shoulder. In all fairness to Kristen, I must note that this particular shot was

*Figure One. Photo by Mallory Thomas Taulbee of Avia Photography*

*Figure Two. Photo by Mallory Thomas Taulbee of Avia Photography*

taken in a photo call, not in performance, where her physicality was quite consistent. Figure three again shows Kristen with a lowered center of gravity. Note the curve of the upstage leg cuts off at the waist.

From the point of view of Laban work, much of this physical exploration may be seen as taking place under the aspect of effort or filling body, shape, and space, with feeling, but doing so in a way less threatening than by directly addressing emotion itself (Adrian 3074). Regarding Laban's effort factors of flow, weight, and time: in flow, operating on a continuum between action that is bound and that which is free, masculine action might be thought of as gravitating more towards the pole of behavior that is condensed and ready to fight. Certainly this seems to be the case for Kent. However, Greg may be seen initially as being closer to the unbound pole of the continuum, especially with regard to his speech, moving strongly towards the bound aspect in his fight with Kent and then back again to a happier medium between bound and constrained, afterwards. While Kent, as a result of losing the fight, becomes less condensed and more diffused in the humiliation of defeat.

*Figure Three. Photo by Mallory Thomas Taulbee of Avia Photography*

With regard to Laban's concept of weight, the intention of the force with which we carry ourselves on a continuum between strong and light, Kent spends most of the play within various aspects of the strong pole of the continuum. However, Greg, for the most part, occupies a more middling area of the continuum frequently referred to as passive weight. He tends to ultimately give in to whatever obstacle he encounters, rather than resist it. However, as with the previous effort factor of flow, in the course of the play, Greg moves towards strong and condensed action in the fight and then pulls back to a stronger, but less condensed position afterwards, while Kent's progression is the opposite. Regarding the factor of one's attitude towards their location within a continuum between direct and indirect action, masculine behavior probably falls more towards the direct pole. However again, Greg may be thought of as being more indirect and diffused through much of the play and grows more direct as it progresses, while Kent's journey is more the reverse of this action. With regard to the final effort factor of time, or one's attitude toward the degree of leisure or urgency with which decisions are made, existing on a continuum between sustained and quick, Kent tends toward masculine decisiveness (to do something even if it's wrong) until his impulsiveness leads to disaster in the fight and he experiences sustained feelings of humiliation and defeat. Greg's journey through the play is again, largely the reverse of this. In the beginning he would perhaps like to be quick and decisive, but has no real sense of urgency about anything and is continually humiliated. As the circumstances of his life grow more urgent, he begins to respond more quickly, then retreats to a more moderate, but still relatively urgent stance.

Laban technique is productive because it provides a means of expression and common vocabulary for actors and directors; I suspect Viewpoints would serve the same function as well. Michael Chekov's exercises exploring the Imaginary Body, Imaginary Center, and the connection of mind and body are also intriguing ways to explore the essential differences in how gender may be embodied (Petit 93-97, 107-115). Most useful of all perhaps are William Esper's exercises incorporating the imitation of someone known to, or observed by, the actor. The actor strives to "do a perfect imitation, not a lampoon or a caricature" with the ultimate goal of truthfully altering their natural behavior in a way that affects them internally as well, but without negatively impacting the improvisatory mindset of moment-to-moment reality (Esper 74-75, 84-85).

Gauging the success of any production, especially when the critic is its director, is a tenuous process. However, there is also something to be said for the point of view that maintains, "Who should know better?" For myself, all I can say is that as an audience member I tend to be both hyper-critical and easily bored and this production held my attention and made me think every time I saw it. Once the audience adjusted to the unfamiliar casting, the difference between the gender of the actor and that of the character faded from attention and the spectators were free to accept or reject the play and production as being worthy of their time or not. For me, the biggest discovery to emerge from this production is, in the end, how little difference the perceived gender of an actor actually makes, as opposed to their talent, skill, commitment, and courage. However, more than one person whose opinion in these matters I respect maintains that they enjoyed our production more than they admired the play itself. Most felt that this was directly due to women actors playing masculine characters who are maddening, in Greg's case, and blatantly misogynistic and racist in Kent's. My friend and colleague, Dr. C. Francis Blackchild, described this as "a very liberating thing." To me, this simply reinforces my belief in casting the best actors who are best together, regardless of either their own or the character's gender.

The concept of women actors playing masculine characters, as intended by the playwright, is straightforward and transparent. It is a relatively simple matter to frame the gender of a character as another aspect of the play's given circumstances and treat it as such in the casting process. While this may well lead to conflict with the intentions of the playwright, there is an argument to be made that since neither the gender of the character nor the text has been altered, the only real difference is the gender of the actor traditionally associated with the role. If the playwright truly believes that this is a significant enough factor and objects, then obviously, their intellectual property rights must be upheld. However, even in this instance, there is the possibility of a productive and illuminating conversation about the nature of the play and its realization in performance, and as these conversations multiply, our consciousness regarding these and other issues may expand. By setting aside the gender of the actor traditionally identified with a character, we address the overall dearth of substantial roles for women actors. As a result, the classical as well as the contemporary repertory is dramatically expanded. Furthermore, this practice encourages both actor and audience to speculate and imagine, rather than to simply identify or not, with any given play or character. The nature of the process by which we pick sides and root for our team without reflection is exposed and made conscious. These aspects allow us to experience the realities of dominant power in culture, even if we ourselves occupy a position within it and even if we have difficulty acknowledging that membership.

## Works Cited

Adrian, Barbara. *Actor Training the Laban Way: An Integrated Approach to Voice, Speech, and Movement.* Allworth Press. Kindle Edition, 2010.

Brecht, Bertolt. *Brecht on Performance: Messingkauf and Modelbooks. Performance Books.* Bloomsbury Publishing. Kindle Edition, 2014.

Carnicki, Sharon. *Stanislavsky in Focus.* New York: Routledge, 2014.

Esper, William and Damon DiMarco. *The Actor's Guide to Creating a Character.* New York: Anchor Books 2014.

LaBute, Neil. *Reasons to be Pretty.* New York: Dramatists Play Service, 2009.

Petit, Lenard. *The Michael Chekhov Handbook: For the Actor.* Taylor and Francis. Kindle Edition, 2009.

Schechner, Richard. "Casting Without Limits." *American Theatre,* December. 2010.

# More Than Games: Integrating Improvisation with Stanislavski-based Actor Training
*Tom Smith*

In undergraduate actor training, improvisation is often treated as supplemental and rarely introduced or integrated as a vital pedagogical component. It is usually relegated to short games or exercises to build trust among the class during the first few weeks, then dropped completely to allow enough time for "real" acting skills to be introduced and developed. Even in survey courses, the definition of theatre traditionally includes written scripts, consigning improvisation to performance rather than theatre (Hischak 2-3). Therefore, it should not be surprising to discover that most acting students are undertrained in improvisation and view it as a boutique skill rather than a core element in their training. In my first semester teaching at New Mexico State University, I was challenged for "excessively" teaching improvisation in my beginning acting course. But I was using the lens of improvisation to not only teach basic performance values, as my colleagues did, but also as a means to teach Stanislavski-based methodology. My colleagues saw no connection between the two but became curious after seeing positive results from my students. This encouraged me to focus my scholarship on defining the tightly-knit relationship between these distinct but similar approaches to actor training.

Historically, improvisation has been performed for hundreds of years. Although most credit Commedia dell'Arte with popularizing it, one would be hard-pressed to not consider some of the earliest forms of theatre utilizing improvisation, especially the broad farce of Roman theatre. In America, improvisation was used throughout the twentieth century in programs designed to facilitate creative play and childhood development, such as in the work of Viola Spolin, and presented as its own form of entertainment by companies such as

Second City and IO. There was considerable growth in improvisation in the 1980s when stand-up comedy and a large number of comedy clubs and television programs presented comedy shows regularly (Bromley). Short-form improvisation, with its quirky games and comic bent, seemed a natural extension of stand-up and scores of improv companies began cropping up across the United States during the 1980s, 1990s, and 2000s (Improv Comedy Clubs).

Short-form improvisation proved popular with younger theatre-goers, and improv companies reached out to their target audience by offering multiple hour-long performances, late night curtain times and inexpensive ticket prices (Adcock). However, low-cost tickets meant that many companies struggled to pay their rent. To make up for this shortfall, they began offering training programs to supplement their income (Waldemar). Though each company approached training slightly differently, a core vocabulary and theory began to emerge which has shaped and solidified the modern pedagogy of improvisation. This terminology and performance theory has been available for more than fifty years, yet many acting teachers either do not know it or are untrained in how best to utilize it. These common terms and theories include:

**Platform:** the given circumstances of a scene. These should be stated as early in the scene as possible so the audience and your acting partners know what's going on. Pillars of a strong platform include addressing who you are, where you are, and what your characters are doing (Improv Glossary).

**Bid or Offer:** an idea. Usually the first line of the scene, called an opening bid, sets up the platform. The opening bid sets up the scene while more bids are offered throughout the scene to progress the plot. General bids like, "Hello!" are less dynamic/useful/interesting than specific bids like, "Son, what is that lion doing in your bedroom?" (Schaeffer).

**Blocking/Agreeing:** perhaps the best known and most basic concept in improvisation. Blocking is saying no to, or refuting, a bid. Agreeing is saying yes to, or accepting, a bid. Improvisers are taught to avoid blocking and agree to bids: doing so encourages action and moves the scene forward. In simplest terms: always say "yes" (Johnstone Impro 94).

**Wimping:** ignoring a bid because you either don't like it or didn't hear it. Wimping should be avoided (Johnstone Impro 114).

**Waffling**: talking about a bid but not actually doing the bid. Improvisers are taught that physical, emotional, or psychological action makes for a better performance and that it is always preferable to show something onstage rather than simply talk about it. Waffling should also be avoided (Smith 30).

**Expanding "Yes, And…":** accepting and building on a bid. In improv, the goal for effective performance is basically this: accept your partner's bid, then add something to it. The easiest way to accomplish this is to start your reply with the words "Yes, and…". Expanding moves the plot forward, heightens stakes, and allows more give and take amongst the performers (Smith 34; Halpern 49).

If nothing else, acting instructors can take these six basic terms and side-coach improvised scenes with them. They should immediately begin to see work that produces more active choices and demonstrates better partnering. What causes most improvised scene work to fail or feel tedious is when the instructor offers no side-coaching: students are asked to go on stage and make something up with no guidance. What usually happens in these circumstances is that one actor blocks bids provided by the scene partner and earns laughs from the sense of superiority that has been established. Feeling confident, that actor then continues to block to get more laughs. But these laughs are always short-lived because the joke is the same and the scene becomes tedious. Sensing this, the instructor ends the scene. So what have the students gained from this? One learns that laughs stop quickly and there is no way to salvage a scene so you should just end it; their partner has learned that they never want to work with the first actor again since every bid was rejected. Unfortunately, this scenario speaks to why most instructors cover improvisation for such a limited time: they simply don't know what to do to make the scenes better, much less truthful and compelling, so they give up and move on to scripted scene work instead.

In addition to specific terminology, improvisation includes performance theory intended to make scenes more entertaining and sustainable. This includes Commit to everything: every character, every moment, and every idea. See it through to its logical conclusion, no matter how illogical it may seem. Avoid ironic detachment or commenting on the scene (Buck).

**Play to the top of your intelligence:** This does not mean rattling off things the actor is knowledgeable about; rather, it means adding insight to a moment based on personal experience or expertise. It also means behaving the way the character would behave, knowing what the character would know and being truthful. If the character is an expert on contract law, for example, and the performer playing that character also happens to be an expert on contract law, the performer should use that knowledge to make the character more specific. They should not shy away from using what they know for fear it might be over the heads of the audience. Simply put, there is no need to dumb anything down simply to appease the audience (Besser, Roberts, Walsh 50).

**Object work:** Interact with your environment which, because the scenes are improvised, does not exist. Create a sense of the non-realized set and costumes by acknowledging, using, and being consistent with them. If you trip over an imaginary rug in a scene, for example, remember where it was and trip over it again later. If the scene takes place in 1860, be sure to flip the imaginary tails on your coat when you sit or lift your skirt as you climb stairs. Improvisers must be designers as well as performers (Besser, Roberts, Walsh 27).

**Listen and callback:** To create a cohesive scene, listen to all pieces of information you or your partner provides so you can be accurate when referring to them again. Calling back a piece of specific information accurately later in the scene elicits a strong response from the audience and adds a sense of specificity and credibility to the scene (Smith 70).

**Define relationship and status:** Focusing on the social dynamics between characters makes them specific and varied. The more detailed an actor can make the character, the more impressive and interesting that performance will be to the audience, and the easier it will be for the actor to portray that character (Johnstone Impro 34).

**Make everything believable:** No matter what the bid or how exaggerated or absurd it seems, react believably to it given the circumstances and the character. This adds truth to the performance (Halpern 72).

**Avoid asking questions, leading the scene, teaching someone something, or dying:** Asking a question puts the onus on a scene partner to come up with an answer, and good improvisers should always share the responsibility of providing information. For example, asking, "What's that behind you?" forces a scene partner to initiate a bid; it puts them on the spot to come up with the answer. Instead, an improviser should make statements only, such as "There's an armed robber behind you!" (Improv Encyclopedia). Conversely, leading the scene occurs when one performer makes most of or all the bids, forcing the scene partner to do what they are told. This makes scenes feel very lopsided. Audiences wonder how the other character is contributing to the scene or why they are even there at all (Smith 10). Teaching someone or demonstrating something in a scene—like a scene that takes place in a cooking class—is based on the premise that a scene partner's character will know nothing so they will be hard-pressed to contribute anything meaningful to the scene (Besser, Roberts, Walsh 208). Finally, dying in a scene is the ultimate form of blocking: after all, how can you contribute anything meaningful if your character is dead (Smith 73)?

Depending on the specific school of improvisation, there are scores of additional terms and theories. There is also variant terminology used to represent the same idea. However, the core tenets of improvisation are fairly similar among the varied companies and prove to be invaluable tools to help students perform more confidently and make their scenes more entertaining.

One brief side-note: Improvisation is conventionally divided into two distinct forms: short-form, consisting of short—usually less than five minute—scenes in which there is some kind of required external stimulus and long-form, lengthier scenes or even entire plays that use external stimuli but often on a more limited basis. For example, in the short-form game Alphabet, the required external stimulus is that every line spoken must start with the next letter of the alphabet and will end with the twenty-sixth line. In a long-form piece, a single suggestion might be solicited from the audience to be the theme of the hour-long performance, such as "loss" or "greed." The vocabulary and theories of improvisation apply to both forms equally effectively, although long-form traditionally incorporates vocabulary and theory from the fields of playwriting and directing as well (Smith 15).

In a beginning acting class, it is important for students to be trained in the vocabulary most commonly used by American directors; this tends to originate from Stanislavski's system. While time, translation, and interpretations vary, most acting instructors will cover the following:

1) Concentration: maintaining a point of attention that is within the world of the play and not in the auditorium (Stanislavsky *An Actor Prepares* 75).

2) Observation: observing things in life carefully and bestowing on them backgrounds to help heighten emotional connections (Stanislavsky *An Actor Prepares* 93).

3) Specificity: thinking through moments, creating truthful reactions and being able to answer any question about a moment, character, or object (Stanislavsky *An Actor Prepares* 70).

4) Given Circumstances: fully realizing the physical, emotional, social, and psychological circumstances of the character and a moment (Stanislavsky *An Actor Prepares* 71).

5) Magic If: using imagination ("what if…") to lift a performance out of everyday life and into the world of artistic freedom and creation (Stanislavsky *An Actor Prepares* 51).

6) Objective/Super-objective and Through-line: fully compre-

hending every moment and connecting it to the next moment to help guide everyone towards the super-objective (Stanislavsky *An Actor Prepares* 273).

7) Tactics: the varied ways in which a character tries to pursue and achieve his or her objectives (Gillett 70).

8) Obstacles: the things that prevent a character from easily reaching the objectives (Stanislavsky *An Actor Prepares* 143).

9) Stakes: how important things are emotionally and psychologically (Gillett 126).

10) Connecting internal experience with external expression: not only feeling emotion but showing and communicating it (Sawoski).

While improvisation is an excellent means to teach students performance basics—cheating out, building trust, projection and committing—it may also be used to introduce, define, and refine Stanislavski's system in a way that is clearer and easier to grasp. The basic performance principles that make good improvisation and what makes good acting are exactly the same (Bermant).

One vital thing to remember is that Stanislavski himself was a very strong proponent of improvisation; in fact, it was considered the foundation of his approach (Leep 9). Stanislavski's actors often worked for months before lines of dialogue were introduced to help them liberate the organic intentions and actions of their characters (Roach 216). Yet somehow along the way, many acting teachers have forgotten this and focus myopically on text and text analysis from the earliest stages of actor training.

In a traditional acting class, Concentration is often taught by asking students to focus on their partner and to be in the moment. This can prove difficult for students, especially beginning actors, because their concentration is focused elsewhere: primarily on saying their lines correctly. The focus on their partner is largely geared towards listening for their cue or anticipating how they will react. In improvisation, through games such as "First Letter, Last Letter" in which one actor responds to his or her partner with a line beginning with the last letter of the line just spoken, students experience listening, concentrating, and being in the moment with each other as part of the game. Since there is no text to pull their attention, their focus is entirely on being present.

Object Work helps teach Observation. Too often, acting teachers focus on observing human behavior as the sole means for creating character. Teachers of improv also encourage this, especially since an actor may be asked to play over two dozen characters in any one short-form performance. But improvisation also encourages actors to observe their environment: how the physical world affects behavior and aids in communicating subtext and emotion. Actors without improv training long for the day the set, costumes, and props are complete so they can begin to work with them; actors with improv training constantly work with elements that will never appear on stage and are therefore bolder in discovering their uses during the rehearsal process.

Specificity is introduced in improvisation by introducing bids, building a solid Platform and calling back characters or ideas. In a traditional rehearsal process, directors may ask for an actor to "find a specific moment" where an emotional transition happens, or "be more specific" with physical choices. This puts an actor in the head and, for some, can make the moment feel manufactured. But if an actor can divorce him or herself from the script—be asked to improvise the scene or moments that don't exist in the play at all—often they find specificity of character or emotional transition instinctually. Because this discovery happens through the context of the character living it rather than the actor thinking about it, the moment can often be replayed more organically and naturally.

Given Circumstances is primarily taught through text analysis in traditional actor training, but Platform work and defining relationship and status are more active ways to teach this same concept. Relationship might be hinted at in a script, for example, but improvising backstory or scenes that aren't part of the play may provide valuable details of that relationship that actors can incorporate into their performance. In *A Christmas Carol*, for example, there's usually little text explaining why Scrooge is so unkind. We know he grew up poor and doesn't want to be poor again, but is that enough to make him cruel? In a production I directed I asked my cast to improvise moments from Scrooge's life, things that might explain his nasty nature—not just his miserly one—and they explored Scrooge's relationship with his family. The actors played a scene in which Scrooge's father was abusive and cold; how his gambling debts motivated the abandonment of his family leading young Scrooge to leave school, the one thing he loved, and take menial jobs for equally abusive bosses. With these new given circumstances, the actor returned to the text with greater depth of understanding of what things triggered Scrooge's rage. More importantly, the actor experienced these moments rather than simply talking about them.

The Magic If asks actors to use their imagination and knowledge to consider natural reactions for the character they are playing. In a traditional acting class, this is a difficult concept to introduce outside of scene work. Yet, in scene work, beginning actors are already inclined to think of self—what are my lines? What am I doing with my hands? Where should I stand? How should I react? The Magic If, while encouraging imagination, keeps the actor thinking solely of self. If this same concept is taught through improvisation, through games focusing on status work or characterization, students learn to play a character different from themselves by working off their scene partner. Because of improvisation's much stronger reliance on partnering, skills are developed in connection to the other person in the scene and develop through working with others, rather than working by oneself.

Mastering Objectives, Tactics, and Obstacles can also be simplified when approached through various short-form improvisation games. Objectives and obstacles can be introduced in exercises such as "Scene Without the Letter" in which actors must create a dynamic scene while avoiding any word with a specific letter; or "Scene in Verse" in which all lines must be spoken in rhyming couplets. Tactics are easily approached through a game called "20 Ways…" in which an actor must demonstrate with the scene partner twenty ways to do something, such as "20 ways to quit your job" or "20 ways to ruin Valentine's Day."

Side coaching scenes to Expand/Say "Yes, and…" is the same as teaching students about Stanislavski's approach to raising Stakes. Because "Yes, and" is perhaps the most commonly taught improvisation concept, it becomes second nature for improv-trained actors to add emotional importance to scenes and physicalize the expression of those emotions. This also highlights Stanislavski's contention that actors must learn to externalize internal experiences.

I wish that students could easily absorb and integrate Stanislavski's theories the first time but, as in the case of my institution and many others, Acting I is a one semester course and, although we build on and revisit these theories in later acting courses, Stanislavski is tough to comprehend and implement quickly. What I have strongly affirmed, however, is that improvisation, when explored in-depth, lays a stronger foundation for understanding Stanislavski by offering a second approach to his somewhat complicated theories. In essence, students learn the same acting theories twice in the same semester. They also learn them in such a way that they can see immediate improvement in their acting, which is not necessarily true in a traditional class where students may only have two or three scenes in the course of a semester to explore and implement these somewhat heady concepts.

Without adequate training in improvisation, asking a beginning acting student to come up with a handful of tactics for an objective seems laborious and stressful; with improv training, because students are constantly asked to take risks and make choices, they quickly and easily come up with dozens. There are many additional skills students develop through improvisation that are invaluable in their development as performers: keeping focus, supporting their scene partner, accepting direction, trying something they may not initially agree with, being specific and consistent with characterization, connecting with their environment, and being able to throw away an idea or characterization when it isn't working. Students are also far less terrified should a dropped line or late cue affect a performance.

It is also important to recognize that there are students participating in productions who have never taken an acting class at all. For them, Stanislavski-based terminology is meaningless. Using improv exercises and terminology can often draw better performances from them more quickly than getting them to understand how to define and play an objective. In my own experience this has proven especially true for actors focusing on film, where improvising dialogue is far more prevalent and valued, and for performers who want to do improv or sketch comedy professionally (Haber).

Of course, it does little good to teach a specific approach to acting in the classroom if it is not reinforced in rehearsals. In 2004, I presented a paper at the Mid-America Theatre Association's annual conference and asked a room of about thirty directors how many used improvisation regularly during a rehearsal process. About ten raised their hands. I then asked how many used improvisation in a way other than developing backstory for characters. Only one raised his hand (Smith). This is completely understandable. Directors don't use improvisation widely in rehearsal because they don't see the connection between unscripted work and a rehearsal process that is traditionally script-centric. At best, a rehearsal or two might spend some time exploring without the text. It is also understandable why those who did use improvisation had an extremely narrow approach to its inclusion; they hadn't really been exposed to its range. But incorporating improvisation games, exercises, and approaches not only supplements a rehearsal process, but has been proven to play a pivotal part in advancing the cast's performances.

I have used short improv games in rehearsals to break the ice, to create a sense of unity, to promote physically communicating emotional transitions and to embolden performers. I have used improvised scene work to flesh out backstory, physicalize characterizations, and refine moments. I have used improv theory to help actors explore given circumstances and exposition and used object work to create a stronger connection between performer and design elements. Some of these approaches have worked incredibly well, while others worked on a more limited scale. However, all have worked; I have never had an experience in which the improv work we did was not influential in the final production. Never once did I feel that I was "sacrificing" rehearsal time for these activities; rather, the time and space allotted for these exercises often got us places more quickly than if we rehearsed traditionally.

Regardless of the limited definition provided in some theatre survey courses, improvisation is not only theatre but is, in fact, an invaluable component of actor training. The increase of alternative directorial approaches that incorporate improvisation, including Meisner and Viewpoints, the need for actors skilled in improvisation for experiential scenario-based plays such as Sheer Madness and Tony and Tina's Wedding, and the recent influx of performances where the audience itself offers an element of improvisation by exploring the performance space as they wish, such as in Punchdrunk's 2011 production Sleep No More, calls for modern actor training to include a more substantial and serious experience with improvisation.

In this ever-evolving art form, especially with its frequent overlapping of film, television, and the Internet, actor training must evolve to better prepare students for the demands of new media and changing theatrical forms. It is imperative that we reframe our thinking of improvisation as less a boutique skill we use to warm up the class and more as a pedagogically sound and necessary component of every actor's training.

## Works Cited

Adcock, Joe. "Innovative Theater Groups Hook Young Patrons with Satire, Sex, MTV." *Seattle Post-Intelligencer* 11 June 2003, Arts and Entertainment sec. Hearst Seattle Media, LLC. Web. 25 Mar. 2015. <http://www.seattlepi.com/ae/article/Innovative-theater-groups-hook-young-patrons-with-1116878.php#photo-633093>.

Bermant, Gordon. "The Relationship of Improv to Embodiment." *National Center for Biotechnology Information.* U.S. National Library of Medicine, 10 Dec. 2013. Web. 02 Sept. 2014.

Besser, Matt, Ian Roberts, and Matt Walsh. *The Upright Citizens Brigade Comedy Improvisation Manual.* 1st ed. New York: Comedy Council of Nicea LLC, 2013. Print.

Bromley, Patrick. "Stand-Up Comedy in the '80s." About. About Entertainment, n.d. Web. 28 Aug. 2014.

Buck, Andrew. "3 Ways to Amplify Your Improv." Austin Improv. Austin Creative Alliance, 27 May 2014. Web. 28 Aug. 2014.

"5 Basic Improv Rules." 5 Basic Improv Rules. *Improv Encyclopedia,* n.d. Web. 07 Sept. 2014.

Gillett, John. *Acting Stanislavski: A Practical Guide to Stanislavski's Approach and Legacy.* London: Bloomsbury Methuen Drama, 2014. Print.

Haber, Paul. "To Improvise or Not to Improvise." Backstage.com. Backstage LLC, 2 June 2011. Web. 07 Sept. 2014.

Halpern, Charna. *Art by Committee: A Guide to Advanced Improvisation.* Colorado Springs, CO: Meriwether Pub., 2006. Print.

Hischak, Thomas S. "The Theatre." *Theatre as Human Action: An Introduction to Theatre Arts.* Lanham: Scarecrow, 2006. 2-3. Print.

"Improv Comedy Clubs." Improv. LaughStub LLC, n.d. Web. 28 Aug. 2014.

"Improv Glossary: Platform." Improv Glossary: Platform. *Improv Encyclopedia,* n.d. Web. 28 Aug. 2014.

Johnstone, Keith. *Impro for Storytellers.* New York: Routledge/Theatre Arts, 1999. Print.

---. *Impro: Improvisation and the Theatre.* New York: Routledge, 1981. Print.

Leep, Jeanne. *Theatrical Improvisation: Short Form, Long Form, and Sketch-Based Improv.* New York: Palgrave Macmillan, 2008. Print.

Roach, Joseph R. *The Player's Passion: Studies in the Science of Acting.* Ann Arbor: U of Michigan, 1993. Print.

Sawoski, Perviz. "The Stanislavski System: Growth and Methodology." 2 (n.d.): 1-26. Web. 7 Sept. 2014.

Schaeffer, Jerry. "The Devil's Dictionary of Terminology for the Improvisational Theatre | YESand.com." YESand.com. Yes And Productions, 10 May 2010. Web. 28 Aug. 2014.

Smith, Tom. "Yes, And...: effective teaching of improvisation." Mid-America Theatre Association Conference. Kansas City. Mar. 2004. Lecture.

---. *The Other Blocking: Teaching and Performing Improvisation.* Dubuque, IA: Kendall Hunt Pub, 2009. Print.

Stanislavsky, Konstantin. *An Actor Prepares.* New York: Theatre Arts, 1946. Print.

---. *An Actor's Work.* New York: Routledge, 1989. Print.

Waldemar, Carla. "At Brave New Workshop, Can Funny Make Money?" Twin Cities Business 19 Apr. 2013. MSP Communications. Web. 25 Mar. 2015. http://tcbmag.com/Industries/Nonprofits-and-the-Arts/At-Brave-New-Workshop-Can-Funny-Make-Money?page=1.

# Theatre as Communication: Performing Arts Training as Foundational Across Disciplines

*Marjorie Gaines*

Teaching performing arts to students, teachers, and administrators who have no theatrical aspirations or backgrounds has taught me to define theatre in the most basic and practical terms. I have to constantly ask what there is about the skills and strategies of theatre that make them necessary and useful no matter what one chooses to do in life. The answer that seems to resonate most deeply comes down to the transferring of information from at least one person to another. If a human voice and/or body is involved in the sending of information, and another human is engaged in the act of receiving, a theatrical-type event is taking place.

When first thought about, this answer might seem too simplistic to describe theatre, a human performance activity that can include and even require special venues, numerous performers, well-crafted scripts, intricate designs, and weeks of rehearsal. Yet even under the most lavish and practiced of circumstances, the event is dependent upon at least one person communicating as a performer to at least one person who is bearing witness on the receiving end of that communication. If either side of the audience/performer equation is missing, there may be activity, but there won't be theatre. As soon as both sides are present, even if only one person performs for one audience member, and they're standing on a sidewalk, theatre is possible.

By this definition, as soon as one leaves home in the morning, they increase their chance of participating in theatrical-type events, or communicating with others through voice and body language. If they live with others, they will most likely engage in these events before they even walk out the door. Theatrical-type events involving the human voice and or body in the act of communication are a daily occurrence for most people no matter what their interests or pursuits. It makes sense to learn how to do something well if done often, yet the study of theatre skills and strategies is usually reserved for those in pursuit of stage or screen careers. Students are taught to read, write, and work with numbers, but the ability to communicate through vocal or body language is left to chance, and is at best considered an elective study. Meanwhile, people who communicate well have a greater chance of being understood, holding attention, and therefore achieving their goals. The importance of studying skills and strategies of theatre performance goes beyond training for a theatrical career, and could benefit any student preparing for success.

Acting, or playing characters, adds the opportunity to move, speak, and think differently about the act of communication. In this way, performance activities inspire self-knowledge as well as the ability to understand different points of view. Strengthening the ability to send and receive vocal and physical information with an open mind increases the chance that a shared understanding through communication will be successful. A breakdown or lack of communication is less likely to happen when participants have good theatrical training. I remember the late, great Nina Foch saying to her acting and directing students that technique is for when the gods don't kiss you, but if you have technique, the gods will kiss you more often.

## Acting for Non-Majors

Many people outside of theatrical communities seem to applaud the value of the performing arts, but at the same time see the arts as something to appreciate or pursue after the real business of life is taken care of. What if perception of the arts changed in such a way that they were considered foundational to the real business of life? Theatre departments would not be in a constant struggle to stay afloat, and more people would be interested in theatre from all disciplines and walks of life, strengthening their abilities to communicate for success in their own fields. Training theatre majors to teach the skills and strategies of the performing arts, as well as acting and directing, would expand their ability to earn a living throughout their lives, and expand the much-needed ranks of passionate and talented teaching artists. Providing theatre strategy courses for students pursuing degrees outside the performing arts could help integrate theatre departments throughout universities, as well as increase audience attendance at theatrical events; everyone would benefit.

However, a shift of this magnitude in the perception of performing arts training as foundational to other majors would have to be preceded by rigorous, focused shifts in instructional practice. Every performance exercise would have to be taught with a specific, practical goal. At the end of a theatre class for non-actors, students should be able to say, "Now I can…," "Now I know how to…," or "Now I understand…" and be able to fill in the blank with a foundational performance skill. If an acting exercise is taught without a specific learning objective, students might have fun in the process, but walk away without acquired knowledge they could put to use in their lives.

Another perception that needs to be examined is the belief that serious learning is not taking place if the participants are having fun. Learning through the performing arts can be, and often is, a joyous experience. Students out of their chairs, safely moving through a classroom in a variety of ways, making eye contact with others, role playing, listening and responding with heightened awareness, can look like everyone is goofing around if compared to a more narrow concept of what the process of learning looks like. But what distinguishes dynamic theatre training as foundational and inspirational to educational goals are not the skills and strategies themselves, but the learning objectives for which they are being used.

The first place this change in perception would have to occur is in theatre departments. Discussing this with colleagues, I've become aware of a concern that widespread training of non-actors might dilute professional levels of training, especially where there are conservatory programs. However, when theatre classes for non-actors are held separately from professional acting classes, this shouldn't be a concern. Performance skills and strategies are similar for non-acting majors and professional theatre majors, but they can be taught differently, and for different purposes. Whereas actors train extensively to realistically bring a variety of characters to life, non-actors train to communicate successfully as themselves.

Another obstacle is the reluctance of professional theatre departments and students to include classes that train theatre majors to teach performing arts. Talented theatre teachers are vital to any kind of performance training, yet some believe if a talented actor learns to teach he or she is preparing to fail as a performer. Of course theatre majors want to work as professional actors throughout their career, but having teaching skills will not preclude them from that success. If anything, it will give them greater insight into their profession and provide an additional option for making a living in the arts.

## Pantomime for All

Pantomime is an excellent example of a performance strategy that can strengthen the mind and body as well as inspire learning. Pantomime involves bringing stories to life through body language without sound, and realistically responding to things that are not really present. If acting can be considered reacting to images, real and imagined, as if they are real and true, pantomime reactions are inspired by pure imagination. This means every move a performer makes with eyes, faces, hands, and bodies is inspired by an image they have created in their own mind. We create images by accessing all of our prior knowledge, finding the picture memories that fit the requirements of the moment, and arranging them in such a way that we can move in response.

Unfortunately, the word pantomime sometimes discourages students from pursuing the ability to genuinely, authentically, and physically respond to imaginary objects. The word can conjure the image of a harlequin in white makeup and gloves in a desperate attempt to break out of an imaginary box, a performance art for those specifically interested in a mime career. The process and skills of pantomime become more attractive, however—even essential—when pursued with specific goals in mind.

Recently I had the opportunity to attend a variety of Tony-award-winning plays on Broadway and was struck by the use of pantomime in every one of them. Whether the performers were ringing pretend doorbells, tripping over pretend rocks in the road, wielding a pretend knife, turning a pretend key, or opening a pretend door, the skills of pantomime were essential to the storytelling in every Broadway play and musical I saw.

As pantomime work progresses it becomes clear that, the more details that are added to an image, the easier it is to authentically move in response to what is seen. This inspires the creation and discovery of even the tiniest truths and possibilities about whatever is being visualized, and expands the use and understanding of adjectives.

Pantomime work can also clarify and create an understanding of logical sequence. If a performer puts on pretend shoes before the pretend socks, or spreads jam on bread before opening the jar, the body will catch them out of sequence. Pantomime work provides the opportunity to figure out what is physically involved in logical sequence. This can lead to increased ability to give and understand directions, tell stories, and write complete sentences in an order that makes sense.

Cause and effect also becomes easier to understand through pantomime work. With every move a performer makes in response to an image, the result of that move must also be created, considered, and reacted to. If an imaginary peach is bitten into, the details of that peach will create a response to the bite that also must be reacted to. If the peach is juicy, pretend juice might escape down the chin that must be dealt with. If a tissue is involved, where will it come from if thin air is not a possibility? If the imagined peach is mealy and the piece must be spit out, will it go in a hand? If so, where next? Or if there is no hand to catch it, what does it land on, and how is remembering that the bitten peach is still in one hand dealt with? Beyond action and reaction, pantomime trains the mind to keep track of, respond to, and handle a variety of details all at once through total physical response. As it is almost impossible to find an activity in life where the ability to create images, details, logical sequences, cause and effect, and successfully multitask is not useful, the benefits of pantomime training become clear. Everyone is also usually having a good time.

## The Value of Improvisation

Improvisation is another form of performance that has a considerable positive impact on people pursuing a variety of careers outside of the performing arts. The skills and strategies of theatrical improvisation enable participants to engage in successful communication by making up everything they say and do in immediate response to what just happened. Recognizing that life is an improvisation — we make up everything we say and do, moment by moment, to solve a problem or to get what we want—the connection between improvisational training and life skills becomes apparent.

Improvisational training increases the ability to quickly access and sift through prior knowledge in order to solve a problem or achieve an immediate goal, a circumstance people face on a daily basis. Because the rules of theatrical improvisation require the participants to accept everything said as true, the process also strengthens acute listening skills. Practicing the acceptance of another point of view, and specifically responding to it while supporting an opposite view, trains participants to successfully make their points in a variety of real life circumstances.

Many of the most popular performers in the world today have strong improvisational backgrounds, and often their ability to genuinely react immediately to what has just occurred is what is so fascinating and entertaining to watch. Even if we do not share the same viewpoint or opinion, witnessing an authentic, honest response allows us to relate to the interaction as meaningful, and possibly even laugh the laughter of recognition. Anyone who wishes to communicate more successfully with others can benefit from improvisational training.

Acting, improvisation, and pantomime are only three examples of a multitude of performing arts and theatre strategies that can provide technique, skills, and confidence at many levels for anyone who participates no matter what their area of interest or career goals. The determining factor for success, however, can be how the strategies are taught, and with what learning outcomes in mind.

## Silence is Golden
*Lee Evans*

## Towards a Definition of Music

The first item of business that I conduct in my music classes is getting students to define the word 'music,' in the hope that a consensus definition will emerge that encourages them to be broad-minded thinkers and thus be more accepting of even non-traditional sounds, perhaps even those such as are heard in electronic and computer-generated music (In this context, I'm thinking specifically of people of a much older generation who may be intolerant of the unfamiliar and are sometimes heard to reject newer, non-traditional sounds with the pejorative assertion, "That's not music!").

My students offer various responses to my challenge, including the words 'rhythm,' 'organized,' and 'sound'. I then point out that while music does indeed ordinarily possess rhythm, organization, and sound as some of its qualities, it also possesses an aspect that students invariably fail to mention, namely silence. In fact, for every durational note value (whole note, half note, quarter note, etc.), there are symbols in our music notational system that denote an equivalent durational value of silence, called rests.

I also state to students that while a fire engine going north on 8th Avenue, responding to a fire alarm, generates rhythmically organized warning sounds, these alone do not constitute anything that anyone can reasonably call music. What's missing is the concept of aesthetic intent. In short, the creation of music involves the *rhythmic organization of sounds and silences <u>for aesthetic purposes</u>*. Put another way, an attempt to create beauty is a significant requirement of the process, not merely the stringing together of rhythmically organized sounds and silences in some non-aesthetic endeavor. Without a purposeful aesthetic component, any definition of 'music' is incomplete and thus inadequate.

## John Cage on Silence

In 1952, experimental composer John Cage (1912-1992) composed a three-movement musical work titled *4:33*, pronounced either "Four minutes thirty-three seconds" or "Four thirty three." The score, which challenges most definitions of the word 'music,' is one in which an instrumentalist is instructed to not play his instrument for the entire work's duration. Iconoclast Cage maintained that any sounds constituted music, even the rustling of programs or shuffling of feet in a concert hall; in other words, ambient sounds, an idea that may reflect Cage's study many years earlier of Zen Buddhism and his belief that total silence was not possible; for even when he entered a sound-proofed room, he claimed that he heard the high-pitched hum of his own nervous system functioning and the low-pitched hum of his blood circulating.

Cage has said that this controversial 'silent' piece was his most significant work. Silence, incidentally, was also an important feature of several other works of his, including *Duet For Two Flutes* (1934), *Music Of Changes* (1951), *The Concerto For Prepared Piano and Orchestra* (1951), *Two Pastorales* (1952), and *Waiting* (1952). Cage's *4:33* conceivably also might be a musical equivalent of, or metaphor for, Cage's artist friend Robert Rauschenberg's "series of white paintings, seemingly blank canvases that in fact change according to varying light conditions in the room in which they were hung, the shadows of people in the room, and so on."

## Miles Davis on Space

In an October 1, 1991, *New York Times* editorial, of all places—(the *New York Times* is known to carry obituaries of significant jazz musicians, but editorials?)—on the occasion of the death at age 65 of jazz trumpeter Miles Davis (1926-1991), he was referred to as the "most influential jazz artist of the second half of the 20th century," one who experienced the so-called "curse" of having felt compelled to change musical direction every time he had reached the apex of his art in any particular genre: from bebop, to cool jazz, to hard bop, to modal jazz, to jazz-rock fusion, to jazz-funk, never settling into one musical style; his distinctive tone recognizable especially for its lightness and relative absence of vibrato, his phrasing, his sense of space, these features having influenced just about every jazz musician who came after him.

The *Times* compared Davis to Mies van der Rohe (1886-1969), "the revolutionary architect [who] preached that less was more. Miles Davis used the same prescription and with similarly dramatic results. He created a thoughtful, understated, minimalist jazz that eventually eclipsed the brilliant but baroque music of his mentor, the saxophonist Charlie Parker…Mr. Davis stayed in the mode of Mies van der Rohe. 'I always listen for what I can leave out,' [Davis] would say. The result was a distinct sound: voice-like, at once laconic and sensual. It spawned imitators around the globe."

Mies van der Rohe was an architect whose work was well-known and respected worldwide for its simplicity and clarity, and so too was the pared-down playing of Davis. Judiciously placed silences were a hallmark of his approach to jazz. In a December 29, 2002, *New York Times* book review of *So What: The Life of Miles Davis* by John Szwed (Simon & Schuster), writer Adam Shatz wrote: "The biggest challenge in jazz improvisation, Davis observed more than once, is not to play all the notes you could play, but to wait, hesitate, let space become a part of the configuration."

In an April 4, 2009, *Wall Street Journal* article on Davis' milestone recording "Kind of Blue," John Edward Hasse wrote: "The slower chord changes, the sparseness of the themes, and the economy of his and [Bill] Evans's solos all conveyed a sense of space and possibility—and thus helped open a door to a new kind of musical modernity."

## Silence: An Effective Tool for Communication

With regard to the subject of acting, it is universally acknowledged that well-placed silences and pauses are powerful tools for generating tension without the employment of words. Knowing when to be silent is a significant skill for mastering the art of communication. As an example, the old-time radio/television comedian Jack Benny cultivated a persona over many years, for comedic effect, of being the ultimate cheapskate. So in one of his most famous skits, he is accosted by a mugger who issues the challenge to him: "Your money or your life!" The long silence that follows, while Benny evaluates the pros and cons of the offer, garners one of the biggest laughs that any comedian can ever hope to achieve.

From an August 23, 2011, Screen Actors Workshop Acting Class piece titled, "The Power of Silence," come the following insightful statements: "Silence is a very effective tool…as it can draw the audience into your performance far greater than dialogue can…Silence can create tension. Silence can create expectation."

From an October 23, 2008, thedramateacher.com piece by Justin Cash, titled, "The Value of Silence," regarding silence in the context of the field of drama, come the following significant comments: "The value of silence…in drama…when used wisely, its effects can be profound…Silence draws an audience in, resulting in a highly focused image of a sole actor. Add stage lighting and the visual picture can be impressive. Often accompanying silence in performance is stillness. These two elements sometimes go hand in hand and complement each other. Stillness and silence can create effective dramatic tension in performance…[and] can result in effective contrast in performance. It is this example of light and shade that can turn good drama into great drama…when a moment of silence is so 'loud' in performance, you can hear a pin drop in the house. These are moments of magic…"

## The Pinter Silence

In an early essay, "The Echoing Silence," written by iconoclastic British playwright Harold Pinter (1930-2008), he said:

> There are two silences. One is when no word is spoken. The other when perhaps a torrent of language is being employed.

This speech is speaking of language locked beneath it. That is its continual reference. The speech we hear is an indication of that which we don't hear. It is a necessary avoidance, a violent, sly, anguished or mocking smoke screen which keeps the other in its place. When true silence falls, we are still left with echo, but are nearer nakedness. One way of looking at speech is to say that it is a constant stratagem to cover nakedness…We have heard many times that tired, grimy phrase: 'failure of communication'…and this phrase has been fixed to my work quite consistently. I believe the contrary. I think that we communicate only too well, in our silence, in what is unsaid (*The Guardian*).

There is a famous expression known as 'The Pinter pause' or 'The Pinter moment,' referring to his frequent stage directions that indicate pause and silence, when his characters don't speak at all—pauses that actors apparently often tend to overdo. In fact, when he has acted in his own plays, Pinter is said to have eliminated many of them. Many play directors, however, are known to feel that it would be a mistake for directors to ignore Pinter's pauses, as they feel that his pauses are as significant as his lines.

### The Audience Use of Silence

In the online article "Speak! Fun and Easy Speaking with Craig Senior," he writes that "Random silence confuses. Silence needs to occur just after the words or syllables that carry the meaning, so that the audience has time to respond to its meaning….Pausing is facilitated by word sequence, placing the power words so that you can pause after them. Consider the following sentence: 'I opened the box. Inside I found a mouse, that looked dead…until it moved!' The sequence of words and the punctuation almost demand that you pause. Comedians do this with a joke structure, such as the Jack Benny comedy skit described earlier."

## Silence in Public Speaking

In his piece "Speak for Success! from The Genard Method" [a method of public speaking inspired by theatrical techniques], Dr. Gary Genard maintains that one's power as a speaker flows from the use of silence. He writes: "That's because you must command your audience's attention…You've seen it (and heard it) many times with powerful presenters: a speaker who embodies authority will pause at the podium or the front of a room before beginning. In that moment, the audience attends."

Dr. Genard recommends the following five ways in which to use silence productively when speaking:

1. Pause between the major parts of your speech, in order to allow the audience to process the information you are conveying.

2. Pause after you say something you deem important, in order to allow your audience to absorb the information you have provided.

3. Use dramatic pauses in the same effective manner in which actors use them: to create tension.

4. Be silent after posing a question to the audience, for the silence acts to focus the audience's attention.

5. Utilize silence as a pacing device. It demonstrates the speaker's confidence and masks any possible stage fright or nervousness on the speaker's part.

The bottom line here is: Don't be in a hurry to fill silences! They can be an extremely effective tool in drama, speechmaking, and even music.

## Gary Cooper

The trademark laconic, slow speech and hesitations of iconic film actor Gary Cooper (1901-1961) — personal characteristics which he once facetiously attributed to an inability to remember his lines— very much remind me in those respects of Miles Davis' spare and economical approach to jazz trumpet playing. If one were to think of the words of a play or film as the rough equivalent of the notes of a jazz improvisation, or of the significant silences of a John Cage musical work, the connection between the two idioms—drama and music—becomes readily apparent. Just as Cooper, whose speech pauses and understated acting style came to be viewed as symbols of honesty, authenticity, and integrity, so too did Miles Davis's understated jazz trumpet playing, with its sparseness, restraint, and distinctive tone color, come to represent a comparable naturalness and authenticity; and Davis came to be revered by his peers and the general public as a musician of the utmost musical integrity.

## Noteworthy Quotes on Silence

To conclude this article, here are several keenly insightful quotations on the subject of silence, the source for which is the invaluable website resource *Quoteland.com*:

"There are times when silence has the loudest voice." Leroy Brownlow
"Silence is more eloquent than words." Thomas Carlyle
"Silence is the great teacher, and to learn its lessons you must pay attention to it." Deepak Chopra
"Silence is one of the great arts of conversation." Cicero
"Silence is the ultimate weapon of power." Charles DeGaulle
"That man's silence is wonderful to listen to." Thomas Hardy
"Well-timed silence is the most commanding expression." Mark Helprin
"The learning of the grammar of silence is an art much more difficult to learn than the grammar of sounds." Ivan Illich
"What she doesn't say is just as important as what she does say." Jonathan Katz
"The most precious things in speeches are the pauses." Sir Ralph Richardson
"Silence at the proper season is wisdom, and better than any speech." Plutarch
"Music is the space between the notes." Claude Debussy

In an article in the "Science Times" section of the *New York Times* on November 24, 2015, writer Dennis Overbye interprets and amplifies the above Debussy statement with the following thoughts:

*"Only by the grace of precisely articulated pauses can the character of individual notes be perceived and music distinguished from noise"* and *"Jazz musicians often insist that the notes they choose not to play are as important as the ones they do."*

Here is a final quotation especially relevant to the art of acting, among other areas:

*"The Pause, that impressive silence, that eloquent silence, that geometrically progressive silence which often achieves a desired effect where no combination of words, however so felicitous, could accomplish it."* Mark Twain

### Works Cited

Cash, Justin. *The Value of Silence*. thedramateacher.com, October 23, 2008.

Genard, Dr. Gary. *Speak for Success! Silence! Five Ways to Use This Powerful Public Speaking Tool,* November 24, 2013.

Hasse, John Edward. *Kind of Blue*. Wall Street Journal column, April 4, 2009. *New York Times* editorial tribute to Miles Davis, October 1, 1991.

Overbye, Dennis. *New York Times* Science Times A Century Ago, Einstein's Theory of Relativity Changed Everything, November 24, 2015.

Pinter, Harold. T*he Echoing Silence*, www.theguardian.com/culture/2008/dec/31.

Quoteland.com. Miscellaneous quotations on the subject of silence.

Screen Actors Guild Workshop Acting Classes. *The Power of Silence*. August 23, 2011.

Senior, Craig. *Speak! Fun and Easy Speaking with Craig Senior. Permit Audience to Use Silence Effectively (Pause),* March 1, 2010.

Shatz, Adam. "So What: The Life of Miles Davis," *New York Times Book Review*, December 29, 2002.

## HISTORICAL DOCUMENT

Anna Cora (Ogden) Mowatt was born in Bordeaux, France, March 5, 1819, the tenth child in a family of fourteen children. As a child in France, Anna performed in private productions of plays produced by her older sister. When she was seven, the Ogdens moved to New York where Anna wrote poetry and plays and performed in them as well. At thirteen, she met James Mowatt, who was twelve years her senior. He courted her and when she was fifteen, he requested her hand in marriage, but her father said they had to wait until she was seventeen. Three different clergymen refused to join them in marriage, so at fifteen, they eloped (Mowatt 55-57). Mrs. Mowatt wrote her first play at seventeen and by 1840 had three plays published, though none of them have remained in the American Repertory.

She had also shown an aptitude for acting ever since childhood. But it was only when her husband lost both health and fortune that she turned to the theatre, at first with public readings and then with the writing of a play, *Fashion; or Life in New York*, which opened in 1845 to instant success at the famous Park Theatre of New York (Gassner xxxi).

Though Mrs. Mowatt herself was of fragile health and had a second successful play, *Armand, the Child of the People* in 1847, it was clear from the beginning that a successful play "was an insufficient source of income, she went on the stage" (Ibid) despite the fact that she had never acted professionally. Her first foray into the professional theaters as an actor was in Bulwer-Lytton's romantic play *The Lady of Lyons* in June of 1845. The following document is her recollection of that debut.

# Anna Cora Mowatt
## *Autobiography of An Actress*
## Chapter XII

Preparations for Début. - First Rehearsal with the Company. - Stage Fright. - Star Dressing Room. - Call Boy's Amusement. - A Boast opportunely recalled. - Rising of the Curtain. - The Début. - Second Appearance in public. - Walnut Street Theatre. - A distressing Incident. - Indignation of an Audience. - Painful Discovery. - Conclusion of Engagement. - Fashion performed for Mr. Blake's Benefit. - First Appearance on Gertrude.

The day of my début was fixed. It was in the month of June, 1845. I had three weeks only for preparation. Incessant study, training—discipline of a kind which the actor-student alone can appreciate—were indispensable to perfect success. I took fencing lessons, to gain firmness of position and freedom of limb. I used dumb bells, to overcome the constitutional weakness of my arms and chest. I exercised my voice during four hours every day, to increase its power. I wore a voluminous train for as many hours daily, to learn the graceful management of queenly or classic robes. I neglected no means that could fit me to realize my beau ideal of Campbell's lines:

> But by the mighty actor brought,
> Illusion's perfect triumphs come;
> Verse ceases to be airy thought,
> And sculpture to be dumb.

The day before my début, it was necessary that I should rehearse with the company. I found this a severer ordeal than performing before the public. Once more I stood upon the dimly-lighted, gloomy stage, not now in the position of an anchor, to observe, to criticize, to suggest, but to be observed, to be criticized, very possibly—nay, very probably to be ridiculed, if I betrayed the slightest ignorance of what I attempted. There is always a half-malicious curiosity amongst actors to witness the shortcoming of a novice. They invariably experience strong inclinations to prophesy failure. No wonder; for they know best the nice subtleties of their own art—the unexpected barriers that start up between the neophyte and his goal.

Only those actors who are engaged in the scene rehearsed are permitted to occupy the stage. The play was the *Lady of Lyons*. Mrs. Vernon, as Madame Deschapelles, and I, as Pauline, took our seats to open the first scene. The actors crowded around the wings, eager to pass judgment on the trembling débutante. The stage manager, seated at his table, scanned her with cold and scrutinizing eyes. The pale prompter laid his book upon his knee, that he might stare at her more deliberately. Even the sleepy little call boy, regardless of the summons in his hand, put on the sapient look and attitude of a critic.

*Schlesinger Library, Radcliffe Institute, Harvard University.*

"If I could but shut out all these eyes!" I said to myself. But, turn whatever way I would, they met me—hemmed me in on all sides—girdled me with freezing influences. After we had taken our seats, there was a moment's awful silence. It was broken by Mr. Barry's dignified (he was alarmingly dignified), "Commence, if you please."

Mrs. Vernon spoke the first lines of the play. By a resolute effort, forcing myself into composure, I replied. I cannot tell why, but the sound of my own voice, distinct and untremulous, reassured me. The Rubicon was passed. I thought no more of the surrounding eyes, so full of "speculation"—of the condemnations. I gave myself up to the part, and acted with all the abandon and intensity of which I was capable.

During the rehearsal of the third act, I was startled by a sudden burst of applause. It came from a crowd of actors at the side scenes—an involuntary and most unusual tribute. To say that it produced no effect up on me would be affectation. For a moment my equanimity was pleasurably destroyed. I had tasted the first drop in the honeyed cup of success.

"Go on, if you please—go on," said Mr. Barry, noticing the pause—and I went on.

The play continued and ended without further interruption. When it was over, the company gathered around me with tokens of undisguised interest. From many lips I received the delightful assurance that, if I was not frightened at night, I should achieve a great triumph.

"I shall not be frightened," I answered confidently. "Not be frightened!" reiterated Mr. Skerrett, (he was at that time the low comedian of the Park Theatre): "don't 'lay any such flattering unction to your soul.' When night comes, you will be frightened half out of your senses—you don't know what stage fright is!" "I have a talisman to keep off stage fright—the motive that brings me upon the stage." "We shall see!" was his incredulous answer.

None but actors can throughly comprehend the meaning of the appalling words "stage fright," the nightmare of the profession—a sensation of icy terror, to which no language can give adequate utterance. I have seen veteran actors, who had studied some new character until every syllable of the author seemed indelibly written on their brains—who had rehearsed their parts with the most telling enthusiasm—who gloried in the prospect of making a "hit"—at last, when night came, and they stood before the footlights to imbody the ideal creation for the first time, I have seen them seized with a sudden tremor—their utterance choked—their eyes rolling about, or fixed on vacancy—their limbs shaking, and every faculty paralyzed.

I was not initiated into the horrors of "stage fright" on the first night of my performance. But the dramatic incubus visited me in its worst form on an equally important occasion. Nor was the attack the sole one in my professional life. By what magic the demon can be exorcised, remains an undiscovered mystery.

The morning of my début was passed with my sisters. Scarcely an allusion was made to the trying event which must take place that evening. The rich apparel, spread out upon the bed, received its finishing touches at their hands, and was consecrated by a few silent tears. One of my sisters only—Julia, the youngest—had courage to be present when that attire was worn.

My costume was chosen by Mrs. Vernon, almost the first actress with whom I became acquainted—a lady highly respected and beloved in the profession. Her name and that of her relatives have done honor to the stage for a long series of years.

As we drove to the theatre at night, the carriage passed my father's house. There was a group at the window watching for us. Handkerchiefs waved as long as we were in sight.

I cannot help wondering what sort of place the world in general imagine the "star dressing room" to be. In the days of my nescience I presumed that it was a sort of boudoir, pettily and comfortably furnished, to which the princesses of the stage retired to take their luxurious ease. But O, the difference! The "star dressing room" is usually a small closet-like apartment, with a few strips of well-worn baize or carpet on the floor. A rude wooden shelf runs along one side of the wall, and serves as a dressing table. A dingy looking glass, a couple of superannuated chairs, a rickety washstand—these are, generally speaking, the richest luxuries of the locality. Such was the "star dressing room" to which I was introduced at the Park Theatre. Mr. Mowatt's request obtained for me a liliputian sofa, so particularly hard that it was at once recognizable as a theatrical "property"—a thing of sham, designed for the deception of an audience. I believe even the demand for this delusive accessory to comfort was considered very unreasonable.

I was just dressed when there came a slight tap upon the door, accompanied by the words, "Pauline, you are called." I opened the door. The call boy stood without—the inseparable long strip of paper between his fingers. I inquired whom he wanted. "You, ma'am; you are called."

"What a singular piece of familiarity!" I thought to myself. "It is I whom he is addressing as 'Pauline.' I did not suspect that it was customary to call the performers by the names of the characters assumed. "Called for what?" I inquired, in a manner that was intended to impress the daring offender with a sense of the respect due to me. "For what?" he retorted, prolonging the 'what' with an indescribably humorous emphasis, and thrusting his tongue against his cheek, "why, for the stage, to be sure! That's the what!" "O!" was all I could say; and the little urchin ran down stairs smothering his laughter. Its echo, however, reached me from the green-room, where, after making his "call," he had probably related my unsophisticated inquiry.

At that moment Mr. Mowatt came to conduct me to the stage. Mrs. Vernon, who played my mother, was already seated at a small table in Madame Deschapelles' drawing room. I took my place on a sofa opposite to her, holding in my hand a magnificent bouquet, Claude's supposed offering to Pauline.

After a few whispered words of encouragement, Mr. Mowatt left me, to witness the performance from the front of the house. Somebody spread my Pauline scarf on the chair beside me. Somebody else arranged the folds of my train symmetrically. Somebody's fingers gathered into their place a few stray curls. The stage manager gave the order of "Clear the stage, ladies and gentlemen," and I heard sound the little bell for the raising of the curtain.

Until that moment I do not think a pulse in my frame had quickened its beating. But then I was seized with a stifling sensation, as though I were choking. I could only gasp out, "Not yet—I cannot!" Of course, there was general confusion. Managers, actors, prompter, all rushed on the stage; some offered water, some scent bottles, some fanned me. Every body seemed prepared to witness a fainting fit, or an attack of hysterics, or something equally ridiculous. I was arguing with myself against the absurdity of this ungovernable emotion—this humiliating exhibition—and making a desperate endeavor to regain my self-possession, when Mr. Skerrett thrust his comic face over somebody's shoulder. He looked at me with an expression of quizzical exultation, and exclaimed—"Didn't I tell you so? Where's all the courage, eh?"

The words recalled my boast of the morning; or rather, they recalled the recollections upon which that boast was founded. My composure returned as rapidly as it had departed. I laughed at my own weakness. "Are you getting better?" kindly inquired the stage manager.

"Let the curtain rise!" was the satisfactory answer.

Mr. Barry clapped his hands—a signal for the stage to be vacated—the crowd at once disappeared. Madame Deschappelles and Pauline sat alone, as before. The tinkling bell of warning rang, and the curtain slowly ascended, disclosing first the footlights, then the ocean of heads beyond them in the pit, then the brilliant array of ladies in the boxes, tier after tier, and finally the throned galleries. I found those footlights an invaluable aid to the necessary illusion. They formed a dazzling barrier that separated the spectator from the ideal world in which the actor dwelt. Their glare prevented the eye from being distracted by objects without the precincts of that luminous semicircle. They were a friendly protection, a warm comfort, an idealizing auxiliary.

The débutante was greeted warmly. This was but a matter-of-course compliment paid by a New York audience to the daughter of a well-known citizen. "Bow! bow!" whispered a voice from behind the scenes. I obediently bent my head. "Bow to your right!" said the voice, between the intervals of applause. I bowed to the right. "Bow to the left!" I bowed to the left. "Bow again!" I bowed again and again while the noisy welcome lasted.

The play commenced, and with the first words I uttered, I concentrated my thoughts, and tried to forget that I had any existence save that of the scornful Lady of Lyons. When we rose from our seats and approached the footlights, Mrs. Vernon gave my hand a reassuring pressure. It was a kindness scarcely needed. I had lost all sensation of alarm. The play progressed as smoothly as it commenced. In the third act, where Pauline first discovers the treachery of Claude, the powers of the actress begin to be tested. Every point told, and was rewarded with an inspiring burst of applause. The audience had determined to blow into a flame the faintest spark of merit.

In the fourth act, I became greatly exhausted with the unusual excitement and exertion. There seemed a probability that I would not have physical strength to enable me to finish the performance. Mrs. Vernon has often laughingly reminded me how she shook and pinched me when I was lying, to all appearance, tenderly clasped in her arms. She maintains that, by these means, she constantly roused me to consciousness. I am her debtor for the friendly pinches and opportune shakes.

In the fifth act, Pauline's emotions are all of calm and abject grief—the faint, hopeless struggling of a broken heart. My very weariness aided the impersonation. The pallor of excessive fatigue, the worn-out look, tottering walk, and feeble voice suited Pauline's deep despair. The audience attributed to an actor's consummate skill that which was merely a painful and accidental reality.

The play ended, the curtain fell. It would be impossible to describe my sensations of relief as I watched that welcome screen of coarse, green baize slowly unrolling itself and dropping between the audience and the stage. Then came the call before the curtain—the crossing the stage in front of the footlights. Mr. C led me out. The whole house rose, even the ladies—a compliment seldom paid. I think it rained flowers; for bouquets, wreaths of silver, and wreaths of laurel fell in showers around us. Cheer followed cheer as they were gathered up and laid in my arms. The hats of gentlemen and handkerchiefs of ladies waved on every side. I curtseyed my thanks, and the welcome green curtain once more shut out the brilliant assemblage. Then came the deeper, truer sense of thankfulness. The trial was over; the débutante had stood the test; she had not mistaken the career which had been clearly pointed out as the one for which she was destined.

The carriage stopped at my father's house as we drove home. He had heard the wheels, and opened the coach door himself. Fondly and closely was one occupant of that carriage pressed to his heart.

My sense of distinctive appreciation must have been blunted indeed if his words of congratulation did not fall sweeter upon my ears than all the applause that was still echoing within them. He had witnessed the performance from a private box, but I had not been aware of his presence.

The next morning the press were unanimous in commendation. The journals of the day were filled with gratifying predictions—prophesies that have not remained wholly unrealized. Offers of engagements in all the principal theatres throughout the Union now poured in upon us. The first engagement that we accepted was at the Walnut Street Theatre, Philadelphia, where *Fashion* had been produced.

I made my appearance there a few nights after my début in New York. If I had abundant cause of gratitude and self-congratulation on the first night of my appearance in public, I suffered enough upon the second to atone for all the elation or vanity of which I may have been guilty.

Mr. C's contract stipulated that he should play opposite characters to me in whatever theatre we appeared. Mr. Wheatley was an established favorite at the Walnut Street Theatre. He had enacted, to the satisfaction of the audience, the same role that Mr. C was called upon to assume. The manager remonstrated at Mr. Wheatley's being displaced; various friends assured us that the public would demand him as my support; but what could be done? Mr. C had the right of supporting me by contract; he could not be asked to forego a right so advantageous. Had he been asked, he would certainly have given an indignant refusal.

The play was the *Lady of Lyons*. The house was crowded to its utmost capacity. For the second time I took my seat upon the small sofa to represent Pauline Deschappelles. The curtain rose. The welcome was fully as cordial as in New York. The first act and the second act passed off uninterruptedly as before. In the third, Pauline is thrown constantly with Claude. I observed that Mr. C hesitated in the words of his part; now and then he spoke in a thick voice; he walked with an unsteady step; and when the business of the play required him to take my hand, his own trembled violently. "This is what actors call 'stage fright'" was my internal reflection; "he knows that the audience desire Mr. Wheatley in this part; and he is so much alarmed that he cannot act."

This misplaced emotion, as I thought it, on the part of Claude, distracted my attention, and prevented my identifying myself with the character of Pauline.

In the fourth act, during the scene between the widow and Pauline, Beauseant and Pauline, I began to recover my suspended faculties. Claude enters; and with the first words he uttered came that sound, more fearful than all others to an actor's ears—a hiss—a faint one, still a hiss! I heard Claude groan and ejaculate something in an undertone. I felt indignant at the want of generosity displayed by the audience. As the act advanced, the hisses were repeated whenever he spoke. A succession of false notes in a concert could not have a more jarring effect upon the nerves. I could scarcely remember a line of my part, and, immediately after the curtain fell, had not the slightest recollection how the act ended.

After a change of attire, Pauline appears alone in the fifth act. When the scene opened, the audience loudly testified their greeting that no share of their displeasure was intended for me. I was too much agitated to attempt to personate Pauline as I had on a previous occasion. I mechanically uttered the words of the text. The anticipation of Claude's appearance, which must take place in a few moments, had filled me with dread—a fear that was too well founded. The audience allowed him to enter, and were silent. Pauline makes her appeal to Colonel Damas; Claude advances, and she approaches him. Without looking at him, I hurried over the language of the part, not waiting for his few words of reply, and turned to the table, where the father and mother of Pauline were seated. Then Claude must speak. The hisses of the audience were deafening. The theatre seemed suddenly filled with snakes. I turned round instinctively; the pit had risen in a body with evident intention of violence. (I afterwards heard that they were prepared to fling brickbats at the offending Claude.) I did not suspect in what manner Mr. C had deserved their displeasure. That he chanced to be an Englishman was, I imagined, his principal crime; and the audience chose that I should appear with my own countryman, Mr. Wheatley, their avowed favorite.

Advancing to the front of the stage, I rapidly entreated their forbearance. What I said I have not the remotest idea; for I acted on impulse, and under a strong excitement, believing that I was only preventing a gross injustice. Instantaneously every seat was resumed. A dead silence prevailed while I spoke, and applause took the place of hisses. There were too many true gentlemen present for Mr. C to have any thing further to fear, little as he merited the defence. A faint attempt was made to conclude the play. The audience offered no opposition, and in a few minutes the curtain fell.

I was unwilling to respond to the "call," but yielded to the request of the managers. Mr. C offered to lead me out. I knew that it was unwise to accept his services, but I could not refuse them without wounding him more deeply. He stooped to gather the bouquets with which the audience, in anticipation of a performance very different from the one they had witnessed, came supplied. Then I noticed that he reeled from side to side, and, after bending down, could scarcely regain his equilibrium. I thought it was very strange that his "stage fright" deprived him of the faculty of moving about without staggering, when the play was ended. The instant we were behind the scenes again, he gave way to an extravagant burst of grief, and darted off, followed by several of his friends.

Mr. Mowatt was leading me to my dressing room when I overhead the Madame Deschappelles of the evening say to another lady, "He got no more than he deserved—I wish they brickbated him—the man was as drunk as he could be!" "What a shame!" I involuntarily exclaimed, turning to Mr. Mowatt; "did you hear what that woman said?" "Yes," he replied, "and it is too true. I saw you did not suspect his situation, and purposely left you in ignorance."

Suspect it? The idea that he was intoxicated never once entered my head. Nor was it remarkable that I should not have recognized the workings of the enemy which "men put in their mouths to steal away their brain;" for up to that period it had been my fortune to witness few similar exhibitions. The painful impressions of that wretched night very nearly gave me a distaste for the profession—but I had not entered it for amusement.

The next night Mr. C made an apology to the audience, stating that he had been led into an unwonted indiscretion while "dining out," and entreating their indulgence. They pardoned him nominally, but rarely bestowed upon his best efforts any evidence of approval. The engagement was a trying one, and I rejoiced when it was concluded. The houses were but half filled, and I labored under a sense of depression which nothing could remove.

At the close of the fortnight Mr. C returned to New York, and I remained one night in Philadelphia to appear for the benefit of Mr. Blake, the stage manager. He selected *Fashion* as the play to be represented, and persuaded me to enact Gertrude. The character affords no opportunity for the display of dramatic abilities, and I reluctantly consented. Once more an audience as fashionable and as crowded as the one which witnessed the miseries of my first night in Philadelphia graced the theatre. Mr. Wheatley appeared in his original part of the Count, and was received with enthusiasm. Mr. Blake's Adam Trueman was more truthful and touching than ever. The play could not on any occasion have given more satisfaction.

## Works Cited

Mowatt, Anna Cora. *Autobiography of An Actress; or Eight Years On The Stage*. Boston: Ticknor, Reed, and Fields, 1853.

Gassner, John in association with Mollie Gassner, editors. *Best Plays of the Early American Theatre From the Beginning to 1916*. New York: Crown Publishers, Inc., 1967.

## Stage Combat Arts:
## An Integrated Approach to Acting
## by Christopher DuVal
London: Bloomsbury, 2016

*Reviewed by Richard Gilbert*

Christopher DuVal's book Stage Combat Arts is not principally about stage combat but rather aims, as he puts it, to explore "acting and voice methods . . . through the lens of stage combat" (1). What you will find inside is primarily a manual of exercises for developing the actor's instrument, focusing on the voice. While there are undoubtedly more books on acting and voice than on stage combat, the book's distinction is to use the latter as a tool to teach the former. Viewed from this perspective, the book is very successful.

The book contains four chapters, dealing respectively with breath, intention, voice, and acting. Each chapter begins with an introduction that DuVal uses to contextualize the section within the larger project of actor training. The rest of each chapter includes a series of exercises and video links that demonstrate the exercise or a related concept. A vocal exercise to be performed while doing a stage combat combination might be paired with a video that demonstrates the combat's choreography. Other videos demonstrate Aikido exercises (another art that DuVal brings to the service of actor training) which illuminate the principle being worked on. This multimedia approach is an exciting pedagogical innovation in Stage Combat Arts, providing effective visualization for techniques that are extremely challenging to explain in words, even with accompanying illustrations.

*Stage Combat Arts* is aimed at teachers, not students; the exercises vary in clarity and complexity, and many of them would be difficult for a novice to reproduce simply from written descriptions, even with the help of the videos. For example, there is an intriguing suggestion about how to breathe without moving your stomach (a perennial problem for actors whose characters die on stage), but the instructions are as follows: "allow the ribs to release to the breath on an easy but extended outwards rib release . . . the energetic holding of the ribs in their outwards positions allows [breathing without visible movement]" (171). Unless you know how to do that, the technical terms such as "release to the breath" are not particularly illuminating. The same is true of many of the stage combat exercises, where DuVal occasionally uses terms that he does not define, and some of the explanations of technique would be clear only to someone who already knows them. DuVal is thorough in reminding the readers that if they aren't already experts, or being taught by one in person, they should not attempt any but the simplest techniques being demonstrated.

However, for teachers of acting who have at least some experience with stage combat, this book is a wonderful curricular resource. There are dozens of exercises, covering a whole range of breathing, movement, and vocal work that acting teachers would find very useful to add to their repertoires. The exercises promise to be richly productive in rehearsal, and I am looking forward to trying them out in class. Another innovation is the idea of "breath choices," one of the core concepts in the book. Categorizing breath as "held, managed, or free," DuVal presents these options as choices that an actor might make for different effects. Most acting (and stage combat) teachers tend to discourage students from holding their breath, but DuVal argues that sometimes it is the right technique with which to tell the story. Even vocal strain and distress become tools in DuVal's kit, once he explains how to safely reproduce them without damaging or unduly fatiguing the vocal apparatus.

My one reservation with the book, however, is that the connection to stage combat often seems thin. A set of vocal exercises to be done while holding or gesturing with knives is so divorced from martial intention it comes to seem like "Viewpoints with knives." There is a section on "vocal violence" which is a perfectly useful and productive drill, running through all the different ways the voice can produce sound, but the only connection to violence is that the drill happens to use "violent words" as examples of fricatives, plosives, and so on. Even the exercises involving stage combat technique use unmotivated sequences of cuts at slow speed, with the fighters politely taking turns. This is just the sort of movement that leads to safe, boring partnered movement sequences which could only in the loosest sense be considered "fights." Even though DuVal's purpose is not to teach stage combat, but to use combat techniques and exercises to enrich vocal production and acting, I would have liked to see at least one lesson showing how fighters could present more truthful, powerful, and convincing stage violence.

The few specific combat techniques DuVal teaches are described elegantly. His non-contact slap instructions and the swing-and-miss lessons are clear, simple, and effective. There are also a few excellent deviations from the outdated (but still taught) stage combat methods common in the American theater, which make many directors disdain stage combat. Eye contact, by some accounts the holy grail of safety, gets a much more nuanced than usual treatment from DuVal, who views it as an element (like breath) that actors should make choices about—where an actor is looking is obvious to the audience and has narrative consequences.

Combat on stage presents, in microcosm, many of the same challenges that acting does. Actors are taught the basic tool of thinking about what a character's goal is, what obstacles prevent them from reaching it, and what they will do to overcome the obstacles. Real fighters do exactly the same thing when fighting, and often actors find that aspect of stage combat to be comfortably familiar. Likewise, the illusion of the first time is much more challenging in (and equally important to) choreography, which an actor may have rehearsed a hundred times, than it is in a scene which, in professional theater, might have received fewer than a dozen rehearsals before opening night. From the standpoint of actor training, integrating stage combat as a training tool for other skills is an experimental move that seems likely to bear fruit. *Stage Combat Arts* is a worthwhile first step in that experiment.

## The Outstanding Actor: Seven Keys to Success
### by Ken Rea
London, UK: Bloomsbury Methuen Drama, 2015

*Reviewed by Kevin Otos*

Ken Rea's *The Outstanding Actor: Seven Keys to Success* is the result of his over thirty years of teaching at the Guildhall School of Music and Drama. During this time he has trained over 1000 actors of which about twenty people, such as Hayley Atwell, Daniel Craig, and Jude Law, have become internationally regarded successes (xiv). Rea asks "What were these 20 doing that the others were not?" (xiv). This book structures both his answer to that question and a number of strategies for cultivating that answer in the form of seven "keys" to success for both one's students and oneself.

In addition to teaching at Guildhall and a number of other high profile academies in North America, Europe, and Asia, the author regularly trains corporate leaders. This business-world experience gives the book an interesting grounding in psychological data related to peak performance. For example, the author stresses the importance of a student having a "growth mindset" in order to develop a healthy relationship with risk and failure (xx). Rea does not discount the importance of factors often outside of a student's control that contribute to one's success, such as physicality and socio-economic status, but chooses to focus on the work that can be done in spite of one's circumstances to make a difference to one's acting career (xvi).

Rea's ability to address what is useful for the actor and what has been shown to be effective in achieving peak performance gives this book a unique depth in focusing on practical matters. In the introduction the author states that the seven keys he advocates will not only positively influence the creative work on stage and screen but will also affect how one conducts one's life. The book is organized into three well-written and accessible sections. In "Part One: Outstanding In Your Work," he addresses five of his seven keys:

Warmth, Generosity, Enthusiasm, Danger, and Presence (1). The other two keys, Grit and Charisma, are addressed in "Part Two: Outstanding In Your Life" (173). In "Part Three: Outstanding in Your Career," the author deals with the challenges of establishing a professional acting career and negotiating issues including which jobs to seek, dealing with the media, conquering the pressure of acting for the camera, and many more (235). The book is peppered with illuminating quotes from highly regarded actors such as Judi Dench, Al Pacino, Yoshi Oida, and a number of other recognizable names that lend his words credibility. These quotes are both informative and entertaining and are well-integrated into the author's arguments and examples.

Part One will prove useful to teachers, especially those featuring movement in their curriculum. It offers explanations for each of the keys and then describes a host of exercises that can be employed to develop each quality laid out in Rea's "keys." These assignments range from those that can be done individually to many more that can be done in pairs, small groups, and/or with an entire class. Particularly impressive is the way Rea describes these assignments, typically breaking each into two sections, first articulating the "Basic Exercise" and then offering details (12). His instructions are concise, and he alerts the teacher to common discoveries and difficulties along the way. Many of these exercises find their origins in the work of well-known teachers such as Keith Johnstone, Jacques Lecoq, and others, whom he credits in both the text and bibliography. But the author has adapted many of these core exercises to have them address more effectively the particular key being studied in each chapter. For example, the assignments related to status have their roots in the teaching of Keith Johnstone, but the author has altered them to address the key of Generosity by focusing the tasks more on listening, following, and giving to one's partner.

Though the author expresses a sincere appreciation and respect for master teachers such as Johnstone and Lecoq, his text does not advocate for a particular pedagogy. In this way he keeps his book focused on the outcomes he has established as the keys to acting success. Many of these exercises, and the majority of Part One, would most easily fit into a movement curriculum, but the qualities of performance he seeks to develop will certainly influence a student's scene and voice work as well. It is noteworthy that Rea does not advocate replacing core actor training with a program devoted entirely to his methods, but rather asserts that acting students will need to develop a "strong vocal technique, a released, expressive body, and a coherent acting process" to complement their work on Rea's seven keys (xiv).

Part Two focuses on Grit and Charisma and marks a shift in tone. While Part One appears most useful to teachers employing movement-based work, Part Two lays out more self-driven assignments that students can complete independently of their instructors, and this is where Rea's expertise in business-oriented performance is most evident. Part Two would be useful to a class on the Business of Acting, but also to anyone looking to chart a deliberate career path. This part of the book is engaging and exceeds the superficial writing on this topic commonplace in magazines and on television. The exercises on goal-making, on discovering one's personal values, on creating a plan of action, and on crafting a personal mission statement are well explained in the chapter on Grit. Here Rea uses psychologist Angela Duckworth's definition of grit: "the capacity for sustained effort in the face of setbacks" (176). In the chapter on charisma, Rea first acknowledges the difficulty in defining the term, offering a number of definitions ranging from the Oxford English Dictionary's to our pop culture "mojo." But as Rea does expertly throughout this text, he focuses on what is most useful to actors and within their control; here, a combination of warmth, passion, and confidence that can produce a kind of magnetism (208). This chapter helps the reader understand the importance of networking and gives the reader a number of strategies to employ so that even a nervous person can attempt to reduce anxiety and make the most of any networking opportunity. It is particularly refreshing to hear these exercises applied to situations in which actors will find themselves as they develop their careers.

Ken Rea states that one of his motivations for writing *The Outstanding Actor* was to address the issues he wishes someone would have raised with him years ago when he was first beginning his career. *The Outstanding Actor: Seven Keys to Success* does just that. It is useful, accessible, and engaging for both the novice and seasoned teacher, and it will be a rewarding read for actors and teachers at all stages of their careers.

## The Actor Training Reader
### edited by Mark Evans
UK and New York: Routledge, 2015

*Reviewed by Laurel Koerner*

*The Actor Training Reader* assembles an array of texts by theorist-practitioners of the twentieth century whose works form a canon often referenced in contemporary Western acting practice and instruction. Presented as a complement to Alison Hodge's *Actor Training* (2nd ed., 2010), this volume joins hers in providing snapshots of the approaches to training that currently infuse graduate, undergraduate, and independent programs. Where Hodge's collection is a series of essays about shapers of contemporary practice (Adler, Boal, Bogart, Brecht, Chekhov, Grotowski, Lecoq, Meisner, Stanislavsky, Strasberg, and others) by scholars with the appropriate expertise, Evans collects enlightening and, in some cases, less familiar excerpts written by these key practitioners, with several additions. This assembly of familiar names embodies Ariane Mnouchkine's pronouncement, cited in Evans' introduction, that "theories exist but have been buried at the same rate as they have been pronounced" (xxvii). Here, Evans brushes off the soil, halts the shovels of time and noise, and holds aloft a collection of theories worthy of consideration.

Implicit in such a work is the encouragement to broaden one's perspective in order to examine habits of practice and patterns of belief. Evans urges the reader to "consider a wider view" (xix), a welcome reminder to practitioners of acting who understand the importance of returning to the well. For the recent graduate, this resource may aid in synthesizing the concepts introduced during their training. Additionally, it makes readily available a selection of source texts that any instructor will call upon time and again.

Those who have seen Hodge's second edition in print will note a pleasant consistency of typographical and organizational style between it and Evans' *Reader*. While each functions independently and achieves particular goals, the two are well-paired, resonating together to elevate understanding of the subjects addressed. Evans' expanded sampling of texts omits Maria Knebel and Monika Pagneux while increasing the number of theorists represented from twenty-two to thirty-four, adding Artaud, Laban, Suzuki, Linklater, Feldenkrais, Suzuki, and others.

There is no claim to be comprehensive, and the editor includes a mention of related collections, humbly recommending them while positing his own collection as distinct. Importantly, he acknowledges the book's bias toward Western theater practice, the form's limitation to textual modes of dissemination, and the comparatively small number of entries by women (Adler, Bogart and Landau, Littlewood, Linklater, Mnouchkine, and Zaporah; Franca Rame earns a nod but is not quoted). Nevertheless, this collection accurately reflects the schools of thought in which we currently swim.

Terms like "method" and "technique" are called into question by some of the proponents themselves, and the many dimensions of actor training evade strict definition. However, a clear sense of things can be obtained through the selected excerpts. Organized according to four themes — Purpose, Technique, Composition and Character, and Presence — each section includes an introductory essay written by Ian Watson, Jonathan Pitches, Bella Merlin, and Dick McCaw, respectively. Their writings demonstrate keen awareness of the tides within acting theory that shift according to notions about emotion, the mind, science, psychology, and politics of the body. In keeping with the spirit of the endeavor, these writers apply their personal expertise to locate the included theories within their broader sociohistorical context, identifying patterns and tensions and summarizing without attempting to explain, thus appropriately allowing the reader to interpret the source material.

In keeping with the book's function as a helper to students and instructors of acting, the essays continuously point to a larger framework of thinking on the subject and suggest additional topics for consideration. Questions litter Evans' writing, and a set of "Provocations" follow each essay (a welcome aid to the instructor).

These promptings toward additional thinking, research, and writing acknowledge the limited scope of the collection and catalyze further scholarship. In good pedagogical form, the reader is skillfully led to draw her own connections between concepts. As one reads and responds, ideas are generated that extend beyond what Evans *et al.* put into print.

Additional useful features include internal references, suggested further readings that follow each excerpt, and an index of terms. These serve to support the utility of the text as instructional aid. Interestingly, the excerpts' dates do not appear with their titles (but are included elsewhere), thwarting any urge to immediately situate the entries within a timeline of a body of work or within the context of their particular historical moment that might result in a reductive reading. This freedom from chronology allows the entries to speak for themselves and resonate among thematic neighbors while underscoring their ongoing relevance to the craft.

Evans asks in the introduction, "does it matter…that most extracts are written by or about white, able-bodied, middle-aged, men?" (xxviii), which can only be answered with a resounding "yes." The answer is implied in the asking, but the question feels a bit as if Evans is evading culpability. Pitches suggests that future editions of this reader "will no doubt capture this shift" (57) toward a balance of voices. Given the names of worthy women that Pitches is able to summon out of regret that they were not included (he lists Pisk, Hagen, Spolin, Berry, Bausch, Halprin, Rodenberg, and others on page 57), I cannot help but ask, why couldn't this edition have included some of them? If a broader perspective is the goal, the canon needs to expand, and the editor might well have chosen to act more deliberately on any remorse about underrepresented voices. However, it must be acknowledged that the book's nature as a complement to an existing text means its content is to some degree predetermined.

*The Actor Training Reader* delivers a thoughtfully organized selection of valuable, often less familiar texts by the theorists arguably most represented in training programs at present. It earns a place on the shelf of any instructor, student, practitioner, or theorist of contemporary acting and will prove its use for anyone seeking to view the spectrum of the theories at work therein.

## *Acting on the Script*
## by Bruce Miller
### Milwaukee, WI: Applause Theater & Cinema Books, 2014

*Reviewed by Joel G. Fink*

In *Acting on the Script*, Bruce Miller, professor of theatre at the University of Miami and the author of a number of books on acting and scene study, outlines the elements of an actor's script analysis work necessary to develop a consistent craft for scene study. Miller's book assumes that actors reading his text have already studied the fundamentals of acting generally taught in a freshman-level acting class. His focus is on students at the sophomore-level or above and his objective is to empower actors with the ability to work in any rehearsal situation. Although some aspects of the analysis that Miller reviews would likely be covered in rehearsals with a director or a dramaturg, he stresses that actors who are able to do their own craft work and ferret out choices from clues in the script will be more successful in creating compelling, believable characters. His goal is for acting students to ultimately become "director proof."

In the preface, Miller lays out his thesis and challenges actors to master the elements of acting that can be learned, which is to say that he challenges them to learn the craft of acting. A naturally talented actor will be able to employ craft to utilize that talent more effectively. And while he notes that "talent can't be learned; you either have it or you don't" (ix), Miller's book suggests that an actor without a significant degree of talent can learn skills that will translate into effective performances.

Part One of the text is given the umbrella heading "Analysis." The starting point for an actor's analysis of a play or scene is the story told by the playwright. Miller notes that the story is the force behind the actions of the play and brings the characters of that play into conflict. He has observed that exercises and acting games have not been very successful in developing the skills of young actors in his classes, and thus he focuses more on close study of the script itself.

Beginning with a review of basic terms such as story, through-line, action, conflict, obstacles, objectives, tactics, beats, and transitions, Miller explains how each translates into an effective tool of the actor's craft. Looking at the plot of the script, Miller asks actors to do a close reading to determine the details of how one event leads to another in a sequential cause-and-effect analysis from the beginning to the end of the play. Miller also advises actors to make choices about pursuing a play's actions in ways that are both clear and compelling. Defining good acting as "acting that is believable and tells the best possible story while serving the script" (28), he believes that if an actor will habitually address all three elements of his definition, success is more likely. Throughout the text, Miller stresses that this success can only be the result of discipline and commitment gained through repetition and the integration of analytical skills with all other components of acting. The following chapters focus on strong active choices that help to increase dramatic conflict and empower the actor in "taking control of the script" (89). Miller concludes the first half of the book using *Ten-Dollar Drinks*, a short one-act play by Joe Pintauro, as a script on which to apply the craft elements previously outlined. The simple plot and contained action of the play make it an effective choice for Miller in terms of demonstrating how to apply the tools he has identified thus far in the text.

Part Two is titled "Analysis Plus Synthesis." Miller's background as an acting teacher is evident in this section, and he begins with a survey of the problems actors often bring to a scene. Some of these problems include making the story clear; making the story exciting; behaving believably; listening and reacting in the moment; and using space and props effectively. These are acting problems which actors need to address if they are to effectively use the tools outlined in Part One.

The remainder of the book is devoted to scenes from *Toward the Sun* by Miller and Alan Haehnel, a script made up of two-person scenes with overlapping characters and a final scene with multiple characters. Each scene is preceded by a list of acting issues to be considered by the performers. Following each scene are notes reviewing Miller's thoughts about the demands of that particular text from his perspectives as a playwright and an acting teacher. He discusses built-in "acting traps" in the scenes, as well as specific textual demands that will require the performers to utilize the analytical skills discussed in this book. The final scene, involving multiple actors, is not book-ended with notes in the same way as the previous scenes, and includes the suggestion that an outside directorial eye will probably be necessary because of the scene's more complex structure. Given the choices suggested by Miller throughout the second half of the text, that section might more accurately be labeled "Analysis and Interpretation." Much of work he outlines in the notes for each scene involves interpretive choices of actions, motivations, and character elements, that are creative in nature and that must be integrated into the more objective analytical work already done.

In the Afterword, Miller concludes with an overview of the difficulties his own students have in the process of learning the work he has presented. He expands the focus to include his upperclassmen who are studying Chekhov, Ibsen, and Strindberg, and he outlines how those authors' plays make demands that stretch the abilities of the actors. Miller ends by reminding his readers that he is teaching a set of skills that must be learned through repetition and hard work.

*Acting on the Script* demonstrates that Miller has thought a great deal about "learnable" skill-sets for consistently shaping well-crafted performances. It is easy to understand how Miller uses his text for a sophomore level scene-study class and how he reframes the traditional task of script analysis as a fundamental craft element of acting. While Miller's focus is primarily on scene study, it would have been useful to also present a general template for the structural analysis of an entire play. Despite the admonishment that actors must understand clearly how their characters relate to the overall story being told, Miller does not give a review of the common elements of a dramatic work with which he would expect an actor to be familiar. Standard terms such as "climax" are not identified, except for one instance in the Pintauro play, where that term is used but not defined. Why does Miller label that moment as the climax? How does it relate to the completion of the protagonist's objective? Even if only included in the introductory chapters as a concise review, the value of Miller's book would have been enhanced if actors could more easily relate the analytical work they are doing on their own roles in scene work to the overall structure of a full-length play.

Moreover, Miller gives no examples of how to use his method of analysis working with plays written before the second half of the nineteenth century and the advent of realism. It is not clear if he believes that his analytic method will work for Greek tragedies or for Shakespeare's plays, as well as for the types of subtextually-based modern drama he uses as examples. Focusing on realistic plays is certainly appropriate for a book geared to the needs of a scene-study class on the sophomore or upper class level. It would have been useful, however, for Miller to articulate similarities and/or differences in the analytical craft work an actor might employ for the many centuries of drama preceding realism.

It would also have been helpful to include suggestions for scenes to work on from plays other than the short play by Pintauro and that co-written by Miller. While the scenes provided by the author were specifically chosen for their value in implementing the craft techniques he is teaching, it would have been beneficial for the book to include a list of published scenes the author feels would offer similar challenges. This type of resource would be valuable for student actors in picking appropriate scene material as well as for teachers looking for scripts that will help exercise the book's analytical and interpretative skills.

As a teacher of both script analysis and acting in a conservatory-style program, I have had the ongoing experience of students taking the script-analysis course wanting immediately to put it into a closet marked "academic class." I begin the first session by suggesting that they think of our class as an acting class and that the skills they will gain underlie all of the work they will do as actors in every class in our conservatory. While script analysis can be approached from many perspectives, Miller's demand that his students recognize this aspect of an actor's work as fundamental will encourage both teachers and students grappling with effective ways to synthesize text analysis with the performance demands of the actor's craft.

## The Right to Speak: Working with the Voice
## by Patsy Rodenburg

2nd ed., London: Bloomsbury, 2015

*Reviewed by Kathleen Mulligan*

Whenever I read one of Patsy Rodenburg's books, it's as if she is speaking directly to me. Not only is it comforting to be reassured that I am on the right track with my teaching, but she says many of the things I say to my students — only she says them *better.* Her passionate, practical approach makes her books readable and accessible, and the recently released second edition of her 1988 book *The Right to Speak: Working with the Voice* continues that tradition.

The book is divided into two parts. The first addresses everyone's right to speak and the many forces that conspire against clear expression. The second is a methodical, easily understandable, practical guide for reclaiming that right.

Rodenburg's passion emerges in Part One as she asserts that all people in all walks of life and in all professions have a right to be heard. She argues that the myths of the supremely beautiful voice and the supremely bad voice are just that — myths. Even with that, she maintains, the voice can be deeply affected by exposure to abuse, trauma, or even the most seemingly benign forms of ridicule such as a teasing parent or an overly critical grammar school teacher. She is a champion for those who are discouraged from finding their voices, and most notably women, the disenfranchised, and racial and ethnic minorities. She does not limit her advice to them but is equally compassionate to the young man who pushes down his voice in an attempt to avoid revealing emotion in societies where men are told that they must be tough. Rodenburg assures the reader that diligent and relatively easy work on the breath and voice can bring about dramatic change in a matter of days. Continued practice can, she writes, create new, more effective habits.

Part Two lays out in methodical detail the exercises needed to strengthen breathing, release physical tension, and place the voice for the most effective communication. Added to these are careful and simple exercises for clarity in speaking. A word of caution for American voice practitioners: her phonetic symbols are based on British Received Pronunciation, and this may cause some confusion for Canadian and American native-English speakers, especially in the description of the diphthongs. On the other hand, a simple awareness of this difference should be sufficient to enable American voice practitioners to navigate this hurdle.

There is nothing mystical in Rodenburg's instructions. Free the breath so that it can support the voice. Connect to the sounds of words and the ideas that those words are communicating. Accomplishing these goals is more challenging than it may seem, but Rodenburg makes the task feel attainable. In her view of things, we were born with free voices and we need to rediscover and restore those voices to claim the right to speak that nature gave us.

There are more advanced exercises included at the end of Section Two for performers and others who make continuous or otherwise extreme demands on their voices. Rodenburg describes techniques for adjusting to different spaces, for screaming on stage, for choral speaking, and for recording. The book ends by addressing general health practices that support the voice and strategies for times when it has been compromised by overuse or illness. Rodenburg offers advice both on what to do if we are in trouble and on what to do to avoid trouble.

Rodenburg's honesty and self-reflection are refreshing. She describes her journey from being "humour-impaired," confessing that "people relied on me for help, personally and professionally, so I became adept at a good discussion but wasn't what you would call a barrel of laughs. I acted in a tolerant manner," she continues, "but sounded like an intellectual snob" (97). From this state, she marks her evolution into being someone who can allow her own sense of humor to come into her voice. "It still gets trapped in the serious middle range," she admits, "but I find that taking the right to express humour will spring it to a higher, more expressive range" (97).

Particularly engaging is her description of the evolution of her philosophy from the old-fashioned elocution of her childhood to the overly relaxed stage speaking of the 1980s, and her observation that the pendulum may have swung too far in that direction for a time:

> When I first started to teach I was too frightened to assert the old-fashioned, traditional view that support work was needed as a daily routine in the life of any professional speaker . . . Unknowingly, I was encouraging disconnection, divorcing the speaker from feeling and experiencing the whole support process the whole time (150).

She now firmly advocates regular practice in supporting the voice as essential to effective technique. She also shares her excitement about recent scientific evidence that allowing the breath support to originate from low in the abdomen actually fires different regions of the brain, and that speaking text aloud allows the brain to more effectively process and deeply understand that text.

In this edition, Rodenburg renews her emphasis on listening as well as speaking, and on the challenges of doing those things in our fast-paced, overly-stimulated society. Furthermore, Rodenburg points out that the right to speak also includes the right for *others* to speak, and that we must listen to what they have to say.

Over and again Rodenburg reminds us that there are no shortcuts. The work needs to be done regularly and continuously if we are to experience and maintain results. Reading this text, I was reminded of something she often states emphatically in her workshops: "You have to do the boring work!"

*The Right to Speak* is a practical, accessible, inspiring guide for the experienced voice practitioner, the beginner, and anyone and everyone in between.

*Great Shakespeare Actors: Burbage to Branagh*
by Stanley Wells
Oxford: Oxford University Press, 2015
&
*Directing Shakespeare in America: Current Practices*
by Charles Ney
London: Bloomsbury Arden Press, 2016
Reviewed by Leigh Woods

Stanley Wells and Charles Ney offer noteworthy additions to the burgeoning literature around Shakespeare in production, then and now. *Directing Shakespeare in America* seems to me to have more immediate uses for working theatre artists, whereas *Great Shakespeare Actors* will draw a wider readership of practitioners joined by squads of Shakespeare lovers and playgoers on both sides of the Atlantic and abroad. Both books compare and contrast past methods with more recent ones and celebrate the richness and variety that Shakespeare productions have shown over time.

*Great Shakespeare Actors* surveys four centuries of performances from the canon. Wells is nearly as Anglocentric in his selection of actors as Ney's directors are rooted in English-speaking North America. Among the first nineteen great Shakespeareans Wells identifies, from the Promethean Richard Burbage to the *maestro* Tommaso Salvini, only Salvini, as the most widely admired Othello of the late-nineteenth century, along with the Americans Ira Aldridge, Charlotte Cushman, and Edwin Booth, owe their origins and their styles to places beyond the United Kingdom. Otherwise, the assortment represents a straight run of greats from the seat of empire and its oldest and closest acquisitions.

Wells' choice of actors from the twentieth century includes more than he called on from the previous three centuries combined. This latter group of twenty draws even more on those who have found their fame in the British Isles. Wells conveys immediacy with his own eyewitness accounts of his twentieth century subset (1). His specificity in capturing their efforts draws attention to the necessarily thin documentation he uses to reconstruct performances by the actors he treats in the first half of the book, in which the entries read more like standard thumbnail biographies filtered through a Shakespearean lens.

It would be ungenerous to quibble with Wells's ascriptions of greatness. But even a meager sampling of performers from other parts of Europe and across the world, especially in former colonies of the British Empire, would have been welcome. Not only have these sites widened Shakespeare's reach, but they have done so in ways that demonstrate the playwright's appeal across time and space and in languages other than English.

Contemporary Shakespeare productions populate stages across the world, and such breadth calls attention to *Great Shakespeare Actors'* geographically-circumscribed sampling. One can understand why Wells would valorize eminent actors who have based their careers in the country they have shared with him and with the Bard. However, another brand of traditionalism suffuses Wells's closer attention to tragic specialists than to comics and clowns. This proclivity has, since Aristotle, left critical accounts and encomia rarer around a kind of virtuosity that makes accounts of riotousness less detailed, even where they exist. The critical establishment has perpetuated Aristotle's bias toward gravity, and Wells's roster of actors, together with their choices of roles, reflects the same priority, one which was probably not shared by Shakespeare.

I found Wells's most synoptic chapters to be his most open-ended ones, including his Introduction, followed, at intervals, by captivating if brief discussions of "Who Was the First Great Shakespeare Actress?," "Who Was the First Great American Shakespeare Actor?," and "Times of Change." The last of these sections identifies staging practices in the late nineteenth century which introduced the sorts of acting we would now recognize and commend.

Wells's long career as a scholar lends his accounts texture at every turn. Actors, directors, and dramaturgs will take interest in the key moments Wells identifies in particular plays, and in the ways actors have rendered those moments, in cases like Hamlet's, for over four hundred years. Even with the reservations I raise, *Great Shakespeare Actors* provides a grand and sweeping survey of one of the Eurocentric theatre's longest and most distinguished stage traditions.

Charles Ney's *Directing Shakespeare in America* uses Shakespeare's motherland quite differently when it acknowledges the influence of British persons on past and current stage practices in the United States and Canada. It does this, however, without conceding primacy to this long tradition, and this serves productions most of us would deem experimental particularly well. The book's geographical compass is rationalized more transparently than comes through Wells's imperial decisions around whom and what to include.

Ney's first chapter, "Texts and Contexts," grounds the interviews by identifying major British practitioners and theorists of the twentieth century and tracking the ones who worked their way into educational institutions and playhouses across North America. The second chapter, on "The Directors and their Aesthetic Values," lays out essential beliefs, some couched as virtual manifestos, from forty-some among the sixty directors included in the book. Capsule biographies set each director's methods neatly into context of the careers they have made for themselves. Ney identifies ones who have viewed the playwright as their "contemporary," using Jan Kott's landmark criticism as a point of departure, and those who have styled themselves as, among other things, "the invisible director," "the language and text director," "the original practice director," "the physical and visceral director," and "the inclusive director." These categories and a few others lay out a taxonomy Ney uses to organize and filter the interviews. Along the way, he has the directors offer a sampling of practices and the premises behind them in what he hopes will serve, in large, as "a sourcebook of directing methods" (3).

His Part Two, "Preparations for Rehearsal and Production," includes chapters on "Developing an Approach," "Research and Analysis," and "Preparing the Production Text," which take up some of the challenges most particular to Shakespeare. The chapters on "Working with Designers" and "Casting," on the other hand, could just as well be applied to many plays besides Shakespeare's. Such generality renders some of the later parts of the book less attuned to Shakespeare's plays as living entities, and it makes some of the directors' remarks seem less calibrated to the play at hand than I assume their productions were.

Part Three, "Rehearsing the Production," treats other issues that seem non-specific to Shakespeare, although its chapters on "Staging the Play" and "Speaking Shakespeare's Language" seem more applicable to his writing. Such uneven focus on what *Shakespeare* demands is compounded, to my way of thinking, by Ney's having conducted his interviews over an eleven-year period. On first contact with the cohort he interviewed, he let the directors speak expansively to questions I'm sure he had broached with them before; years later, he invited them to add further thoughts to accounts he then finalized the year before the book was published. Courteous and thoroughgoing as this is on Ney's part, it doesn't lend itself to sustained discussions of the plays and productions taken up at Ney's urging.

Advantages to this approach lie in each director's speaking to idiosyncratic elements of his or her style and to ways they have, with inspiration from Shakespeare and from their collaborators, evolved as artists. The drawback is that the book becomes something like an instructional guide that would use Shakespearean production as a template for any large-cast or logistically heavy play. The excitement Shakespeare's writing inspires in the directors, and which Ney draws out steadily during the interviews, is muffled sometimes by a survey that, in its procedures more than its parameters, raises similar issues of selection and proportion as the ones I questioned in Wells's book.

*Directing Shakespeare in America*'s final section, "Finishing the Production," includes an especially evocative chapter on "Adding the

Audience." While I wished that Ney had asked more questions on the subject, these passages were most illuminating, for me, when directors identified the sometimes stark difference they found between what they intended and what their audiences had taken away from a given production. Other striking insights are present throughout the book and often offer glimpses into Shakespeare's writing.

It's not surprising that Ney should have begun the book by pointing to the longstanding influence of British theatre on America's shorter history with Shakespeare. The British nation was enlarging its influence, after all, wherever its emissaries introduced the playwright's work to our shores or imposed the English language as a medium for transmitting, publishing, and performing his plays. The United States and Canada have long been postcolonial nations in the deference they show to the mother country, not least in the realm of stage production. Ney's book transposes that deference into a discourse that feels more venturesome, particularized, and assured.

Even with what I found to be a problematic positioning of *Directing Shakespeare in America* as a manual, Ney and his interviewees convey the vitality of performances recreated through the eyes of those who headed them. The range of categories used to focus the interviews may speak to others more than it did to me, but the book records stage practices at a moment in time when some of the boldest directors are relaying their understanding of Shakespeare's theatre by scanning its longer history of production. The territory Ney has charted is made even more indeterminate by Shakespeare's writing having predated directing as we know it. In response, many directors have seen fit to justify an interpretive enterprise which the original productions would have lacked, even with Shakespeare present as a contributor and collaborator.

The parts of the book that deal with "original practices" and the directors who espouse them record the latest attempt—along the lines of building replicas of Shakespeare's playhouses—to stage the plays in ways that don't require any director at all, or which render directors more as stewards and overseers than as creative forces in their own right. Ney doesn't privilege original practices above other approaches, and he's probably wise not to. But present interest by directors in the material conditions of Shakespeare's theatre signals a deeper motive to revivify the plays by understanding them as products of circumstances around their composition and first staging.

## *The Shakespeare Workbook and Video: A Practical Course for Actors*
### by David Carey and Rebecca Clark Carey
London, New York: Bloomsbury Methuen Drama, 2015

*Reviewed by Dennis Schebetta*

In the past decade, a half-dozen notable books have been published with the aim of viscerally connecting actors to Shakespeare's heightened language. Most such books are in conversation with notable teachers such as John Barton, Cicely Berry, Robert Cohen, Kristen Linklater, or Patsy Rodenburg. In *The Shakespeare Workbook and Video: A Practical Course for Actors,* David Carey and Rebecca Clark Carey have added even more depth to this conversation on Shakespeare pedagogy. Without disavowing the plethora of Shakespearean acting training that already exists, the authors stress that actors should create their own unique connection to the text: "there is no universal formula" (14). Instead of a doling out another dogmatic recipe for performance, the authors have created a useful and dynamic methodology that is both an accessible introduction for students and a resourceful guide for teachers.

Both authors have an extensive background in teaching and coaching Shakespeare, most recently at the Oregon Shakespeare Festival. Although influenced by their teachers (Berry, Cohen, and Rodenburg), the authors possess unique ideas and explain their exercises clearly in a distinct, informal style. The goal of the book, as the title suggests, is to offer "a practical course" with the underlying aim to "integrate the technical demands of Shakespeare's heightened language with the aesthetics of those modern acting styles that celebrate a natural, personal, or 'truthful' delivery" (1). The book formulates a three-fold method of working on a text: first, speaking the text without becoming analytical, in order to viscerally experience its vocal and physical qualities; second, questioning the text by looking at word choices, definitions, meter, and rhythm; and third, using that knowledge to "act the text" with playable choices connected to character, intention, and given circumstance (8). Each exercise in the book consistently employs this three-step method of "Speak the Text, Question the Text, Act the Text." The book is designed as a sequence, strategically using simpler speeches from earlier plays such as *Two Gentlemen of Verona* before diving into complex and dynamic language from later plays such as *King Lear*. Most exercises in the book involve movement and sound (such as stomping feet on the stress of the iamb or moving directions when the thought changes) or creative playfulness (such as bouncing a balloon to emphasize ends of lines). The book builds upon foundational exercises exploring physical/vocal choices and developing the actor's intention. From there, the exercises transition into exploring imagery, sounds, and storytelling. And finally, the book introduces meter, rhythm, rhetoric, and their applications to performance. Each chapter explains foundational techniques, expounds on several examples of soliloquies and exercises, and then summarizes the ideas, often relating them to other speeches in previous chapters. Teachers will appreciate the helpful "Teaching Tip" sidebars that appear at opportune moments, as well as an Appendix that includes warm-up and curriculum plans. The videos included demonstrate various exercises being performed by the authors and their students (although disconnections between the book and the videos and their lack of technical quality are disappointing).

The first chapter grapples with "Language and Action," guiding actors to embody the language without becoming overly analytical. The authors agree "that the more precise and clear the actor is in his intention . . . the more specific, dynamic and persuasive his actions will be" (16). Their exploration of speeches from Marc Antony to Proteus focuses on how each speaker affects other characters or the audience. Exercises incorporate movement with intention or explore spatial dynamics to encourage students to experience the vocal qualities of the words. After allowing the student to embody the words, the focus shifts to acting the text, or connecting it to the intentions of the specific moment in the play.

In Chapter Two, "Language in Action: Imagery, Sound and Story," the exercises focus on heightened language and are designed to show how imagery engages the imagination. The authors encourage students to play with metaphor, to embody sounds, and to paint imagery with their voices. The tone of the writing is supportive as the authors repeatedly encourage exploration by giving several variations of speaking a line. Students again work through the three-step method in order to "Speak the Text, Question the Text, Act the Text." The goal is to use language to play an intention with energy and focus. Students who have trouble transitioning from textual exploration to the practical aspects of performance will benefit greatly from the methods that bridge the gap from speaking the text to acting it fully. The authors also empower students to choose their own interpretation on playing an intention, encouraging students to combine their physical and vocal work with their analysis of the language.

Chapter Three covers "Rhythm and Meter." This chapter is the longest in the book and includes material that may already be familiar to students (examining verse and prose, iambic pentameter, trochees, contracting words, eliding, and line endings). There seems excessive emphasis on caesura, but the authors remain focused on the process and end results of using caesura as a tool for actors to interpret the scansion in order to support an acting choice. The chapter uses complex terms that may require further explanation by a teacher; however, the authors excel at providing various exercises for actors to physically engage with the meter, exercises such as rocking the body, stepping, stomping, or tapping tables. This chapter also includes two prose examples, allowing students to explore power and dynamics of rhythm without the dictates of meter.

Chapter Four, "Rhetoric and Style," focuses on the content of the text, using short scenes and more dense speeches to examine how characters "pursue their intention and make points" by using rhetorical devices (182). This chapter explains topics—antithesis, parallelism, rhetorical questions, alliteration, and styles of speaking in relation to status—found in other books such as John Basil's

*Playing Shakespeare* or Barry Edelstein's *Thinking Shakespeare*. The book's examples of language range from comedic interplay to dramatic speeches and illustrate the differences between verse and prose. Once again, the authors use movement exercises in order for actors to understand arguments and how the figurative speech functions.

Although Chapter Five is devoted to "Preparation for Performance," it is really just an introduction to the subject of performing Shakespeare. The authors recognize that each Shakespeare production is unique, from director vision and actor style to playing space and audience size. Therefore, the focus is first on getting actors to explore the technical needs of the physical space. The exercises move on to the development of character, building on earlier analytical techniques discussed in previous chapters and showing how the language is further enhanced by incorporating given circumstances from the specific play. Finally, the chapter guides actors through concrete details of character and performance, such as costume, furniture, and dialects. Although the chapter builds well on the previous techniques, it aims simply to get actors ready for a given performance and thus does not delve into the dynamic aspects of a full rehearsal process.

*The Shakespeare Workbook and Video* should be in the library of every actor who desires to learn or strengthen the fundamentals of playing Shakespeare. Most of the textual examples in the book are some of the most famous speeches in the canon, suitable for beginning students. Although the book is not aimed at advanced scene study, most of its principles can be used for that purpose. The video presentations may be a helpful supplement to the text, especially for new teachers who may be unfamiliar with these types of exercises, but they can seem like an afterthought; often the authors suggest the reader watch a segment without specifying which one might actually illuminate the principles at hand. Also, the production quality of the videos themselves are low, with wide-angle shots cut with shaky hand-held medium shots and inadequate sound, making the worthy content at times difficult to process. Despite these reservations, I would recommend this book for any teacher of Shakespeare, as it contains creative ideas to get students moving and speaking without being intimidated by the heightened language. The authors, just as they intended, have provided easy, practical directions to get actors "out of their heads" and into their bodies.

## *Acting Shakespeare's Language*
## by Andy Hinds
London: Oberon Books, 2015

*Reviewed by Rena Cook*

*Acting Shakespeare's Language* is a fresh, user-friendly hybrid of a book, integrating two strands of practice that are not often dealt with together. The book is one part acting text, one part heightened language analysis primer.

Each chapter has a consistent structure that introduces the concepts, develops them thoroughly with ample illustrations and examples, provides exercises for the reader, and summarizes clearly the key points. This reliable structure allows the reader to browse easily or dwell longer with new information. The exercises are clear, easy to follow without a facilitator, and yield usable and practical interpretation information for the student of Shakespeare.

Several chapters present more detailed information than is typically found in such texts. The idea that all of Shakespeare's sentences fall into one of three categories—order, explanation, or question—is one with which I am familiar. However, Hinds goes into fuller explanation than I have previously found. He provides numerous examples of each sentence type with a discussion of how to communicate the difference in the speaking. Simply but effectively, he explains, "if the sentence is a 'Question,' play the sentence as if the character really wants to know the answer. When you have said 'Explanation,' play the line with a focused intention of 'making something clear' to the listener ... 'Order', play the line as if the character genuinely wants to be obeyed" (7). Hinds' explanation of the distinction between "real" and "rhetorical" questions is particularly useful. The idea that "a rhetorical question needs even more energy"(8) is clear and playable.

An entire chapter is devoted to Shakespeare's use of "thou" and "you," tracing the historical evolution of the use of these pronouns and how they offer clear insight into the nature of the relationship between characters. This is rich territory that is often oversimplified.

Hinds' treatment of rhythm and scansion is excellent. He comes at the subject from several different vantage points, first stating, "that the actor or student does not, to begin with, sit down with pen and pencil and mark the weaks and strongs on the page" (62). He rather encourages a focus on how the verse "provides the actor with the means of getting the character's intentions across with clarity and energy." He offers a variety of exercises that I plan to borrow. "Flashing the strong beats" (71) is an exercise I have already used with actors to good effect. This exercise asks that the actor brings her hands in front of her; she then draws her hand into a fist on weak syllables and opens the hand wide on strong beats. I also enjoyed his discussion of varying degrees of stress, which Cecily Berry refers to as "degree of emphasis." His term "sense units," (54) or thought phrase, is useful and his recommended exercise for playing pivotal sense breaks makes, well, sense. This idea simplifies the term "caesura," and more clearly exemplifies what it is—a pivot in the sense unit.

In books of this nature, prose is often a footnote or afterthought; many practitioners feel it is the less interesting stepchild to verse. Hinds clearly has a deep affection for prose and provides more detail on bringing it to life, pointing out that prose has poetic devices and structures just as verse has. He refers to "see-saws" (175)—two halves which pivot around sense breaks—and "triads"—items, actions or persons presented in groups of threes, which he advises in the playing as "base, build, and blast off" (177).

I particularly appreciated the chapter on "Breathing the Verse." He chooses an approach to breath that marries the two prevalent theories of breath—breathing at punctuation vs. breathing at the end of verse line. Hinds advocates breathing to clarify meaning, which can mean breathing at punctuation, at the ends of verse lines, or at caesuras.

The chapter on solo speeches is highly detailed and specific, advocating several ways of handling soliloquies. One example examines the function of the speech, whether it be a process of enlightenment, a balancing of mind and feeling, or an address to absent characters. He also offers suggestions concerning eye focus for each function.

True to its title, *Acting Shakespeare's Language* is based in solid acting theory and technique, starting his discussion with the importance of assigning clear and playable objectives to each speech. Further, Hinds reinforces that these objectives should be stated in verb form and have their test in "the other" (1). That is, do these verbs have an effect on the other character and spur them to the desired action? The insistence that an objective is not based in showing emotion would make any acting teacher smile in agreement. As a teacher/director I tend to bring acting issues such as this into the discussion once the language is fully understood and embodied. However, starting with acting terms means that the pursuit of objective never gets lost during the process of discussion and exploration necessary to clarify language. Pursuing an objective relative to the other is the real work of acting—expending energy to obtain what the character wants, overcoming the many obstacles that lie in the way. Without it, Shakespeare is just the recitation of lovely language.

*Acting Shakespeare's Language* is an excellent book and would be a fine addition to any teaching library or course syllabus.

## Essential Acting: A Practical Handbook for Actors, Teachers and Directors
### by Brigid Panet
New York and London: Routledge, 2009

*Reviewed by Jenna Lourenco*

Brigid Panet's *Essential Acting: A Practical Handbook for Actors, Teachers and Directors* is the text on acting games and exercises for which many who teach adult and college actors have been searching. Most collections of acting games are geared toward those who teach children and younger teens, and while these exercises are frequently adapted by teachers for use in the adult classroom, they do not generally translate well into the rehearsal room and have a limited range of applications in an adult acting classroom. Panet's games and activities are devised specifically for both adult and college-level acting classrooms, as well as the rehearsal process, though many of them could be adapted to suit younger acting classes, as the author notes in her book.

Panet studied acting at the Central School of Speech and Drama in London in the mid-1950s, alongside classmates Judi Dench and Vanessa Redgrave. Later, she writes, her training continued as she worked in local repertory companies with whom she calls "mother elephants" of acting whose immense talents and experiences were shared by example with younger, newer actors. In the "Author's Note," Panet claims that acting has a more limited vocabulary than one might find in either music or dance. This is difficult to grant, as the vocabulary of acting is shared with many other related and overlapping disciplines, including music, dance, literature, and philosophy. Perhaps, though, one could argue that the vernacular specific to acting is smaller, and possibly less familiar, to those new to the practice.

Other well-used acting texts of this style focus on games to play as warm-ups or activities used to get actors comfortable with the physical and verbal demands of performance. But these games and activities tend to be aimed at younger actors, and offer little insight into how to use the techniques in the rehearsal process or with more mature or experienced performers who require help to find nuances or to break a bad habit. Works such as Viola Spolin's *Theater Games for the Classroom* and Gavin Levy's *Acting Games for Individual Performers* or *275 Acting Games: Connected* are aimed at younger students, and read like detailed indexes. By comparison, Panet's *Essential Acting* is far more focused on providing specific tools for use in both the classroom and the rehearsal room. The book is designed to help the acting teacher (or director) diagnose and treat common issues found while working with adult or experienced actors: creating nuance in a performance, for example, or breaking a bad habit. Panet presents her activities with anecdotal examples of how and when to use each one, and occasionally offers a history of how the exercise was created. This information allows readers to adapt each activity to their own in-class or in-rehearsal situations, as needed. Activities such as "Betty Plum" (32-4) push actors to delve more deeply into their understanding of their characters, forcing them to move beyond the individual scene or monologue and develop the entire character at hand.

The text is broken down into six sections: (1) general acting exercises, (2) physical behavior, such as status, eye gaze, breaking bad habits, and so forth, (3) rehearsal exercises which are explored through Chekhov's *The Cherry Orchard*, (4) specific tips for breathing and for avoiding common mistakes, (5) a section on Shakespeare which mainly focuses on dealing with the language, and (6) a final section on Laban movement.

There are some moments when trigger warnings might be desired, and gendered language dates this work, which was published in 2009. Panet strives throughout the text to vary her pronouns when denoting students/actors, but remains very much in the binary of "he/she," rather than the more inclusive "they" that has emerged in the last few years as the preferred non-gendered pronoun. Trigger warnings should probably be included with any section on status, especially when actors may be asked to actively lower their own or other's status or are allowed to bark orders and control the actions of others. Most of the activities assume the teacher/director will be working in a classroom/rehearsal space of neurotypical, fully-abled students/actors. Beyond comments that only more experienced actors should be attempting these exercises, issues of anxiety, self-esteem, and physical limitations are not addressed.

Overall, Panet does what she set out to do in this text: to provide a more grown-up version of the acting games book that many others have previously offered. This reader has already begun to incorporate some of the activities into her own classes and to recommend the book to students whose work will benefit from it.

## Acting with Passion:
## A Performer's Guide to Emotions on Cue
## by Niki Flacks
### New York: Bloomsbury Methuen Drama, 2016

*Reviewed by Mark Rafael*

In *Acting with Passion: A Performer's Guide to Emotions on Cue*, Niki Flacks offers a personal and radically different approach for actors seeking to produce authentic emotions in performance. The book opens with a series of testimonials from various actors favoring the author's approach. Rebuking Stanislavski-based analysis and affective memory for being overly cerebral and self-critical, Flacks sees "the intellect" as the enemy and looks to the work of psychologist Wilhelm Reich, and her own background in neuroscience, social work, and psychotherapy, as the basis to link emotions to the body. Flacks seeks a means to circumvent the intellect and thereby gain access to what she calls the "Dungeon," or unconscious emotional life. The book ultimately offers a mode of "self-tuning," a process of activating the body and voice through emotionally-charged sections of text. This is where the book veers from addressing the task at hand, meeting the emotional demands of an acting role, into trying to remove perceived emotional blocks from early childhood. What promises to be a practical and theoretical analysis of emotions and how they are produced gives way to a specific, technique-oriented book that is often undermined by its use of exclamation points and bold typeface: "**Be ready to laugh, to love, to dream.** *Unfasten your safety belt* and dare to take this ride from beginning to end. More than anything, you are allowed *to have fun.* **You might be embarking upon a great adventure!**" (9).

Flacks pins the great failings of unsuccessful acting — tension, lack of spontaneity, and self-doubt — on the intellect, the internal critical voice that sits in judgment of the actor's process. As she writes in bold, "**the intellect never tells the truth**" (12). She criticizes the use of affective memory as practiced by Lee Strasberg and the

Actors Studio. She mistakenly conflates the "What if" or "Magic if," tools that Stanislavski describes as a means to enter into the given circumstances of a role, with Meisner's concept of "Fantasy," the imaginative extrapolation of personal events as a means of emotional preparation. As she writes, "The 'What if?' or 'Magic if' actors create *fictional scenarios,* some of which include imagining horrible pain being visited on a loved one: a war, a flood, an automobile accident" (14). She claims both approaches lose potency and dependability over time, citing the natural process of desensitization.

Instead of using visual or verbal stimuli to provoke emotion, she focuses on the mind-body link, relating particular emotional states to parts of the body: "the chest, shoulders, neck and head alignment hold sadness, grief, and disappointment" while the stomach is the seat of fear: "Your youngest feelings—fear of abandonment, fear of rejection, fear for your life—live in your stomach" (19). The face, jaw, and throat form a series of restraints on the expression of emotion, according to the author; the muscles around the eyes developed an ability to hold back tears. The book argues that we all learn to wear a mask and that our bodies respond to chronic tensions and traumatic experiences by assuming muscular "armour." She points to the inevitable tensions between the primitive impulses of the limbic system and the socializing tendencies of the cortex and prefrontal cortex. These primitive emotions, restrained through a process of socialization, lead to muscular tension, the undoing of which, the author posits, is the key to uninhibited emotional expression.

The counter-intuitive solution Flacks offers is to release unconscious emotion through deeply memorized text. She abjures text analysis and physical exercises, at least at the beginning of the acting process, in favor of intensive memorization. By consciously neutralizing fear and self-consciousness through exercise and physical activity, the relaxed body is better able to begin memorization. She also advises that lines be read aloud repeatedly so as to build synaptic wiring in the brain. Flacks emphasizes memorization as a practical acting skill and includes several emotionally-charged short pieces to memorize.

The next chapter examines the connection between acting and unconscious emotions. Memories are, in her view, notoriously unreliable. She again describes the intellect as the socializing aspect of personality that contextualizes information and emotional experience, but that doing so undermines and inhibits the actor's need to unabashedly express emotion. The deep-seated protection of muscular armor must be released if the actor is to gain access to his emotional reserve. The problem, she writes, lies in the fact that actors have negative associations to their own emotions based on childhood experience.

Chapter 5 treats Flacks's process of "self tuning." The section begins by discussing spinal and physical alignment, accompanied by a Vimeo audio recording that reinforces the text, and followed by a gentle warm-up meant to evoke the earliest unguarded version of the actor's self. She encourages the reader to speak poems learned earlier in the book, such as "come here, don't leave me, I love you, please, I need you, I'm frightened" (42), in a childlike voice, not concentrating on the specific meanings but letting unconscious feelings be unlocked through the words. Through touching the face, the chest, and the abdomen, Flacks seeks to unlock centers of emotional restraint. She then talks the reader through a series of pelvic gyrations to unleash buried pain, anger, and rage. The physical exercises are repeated and eventually include text such as, "**Leave me alone. Get away from me. And don't touch me. Get your fucking hands off me! You hurt me so much. I wanted to die. You made me hate you. You touch me and I will kill you. I will fucking watch you die**" (45). The process is meant to unlock hidden feelings and emotions and release them so it becomes second nature; Flacks advocates that readers not listen to their own critical voices but enlist fully in the activities. This section of the book feels like a psychotherapy session or a 1970s encounter group. The phrases she offers don't seem to reflect a universal unconscious experience, and it is almost impossible to imagine doing this work without the guidance of a teacher or therapist.

As she explains in the next chapter, these exercises are meant to give the actor greater access to his or her own emotions. As she says, "**The more you use it, the more quickly and intuitively you will make those connections**" (84). She further states, "the good news is once you're accustomed to it, *being in your body* usually takes less than a minute" (84). However, she cautions against tuning for a specific emotion. Rather, she advocates that one should merely open the door to one's dungeon and allow whatever emotion emerges to shape text. Here she seems to channel Meisner, who advocates letting the impulse, not a predetermined choice, shape the text. Nevertheless, she is still recommending a form of emotional self-generation, albeit different from that of affective memory.

Flacks bemoans the fact that actor training over the last fifty to seventy five years has reinforced the restraint of gesturing, which "has led to whole companies of armless actors, bored audiences and frustrated acting students" (102). She identifies the cause as our habitual fight-or-flight response to the perceived danger of being watched by strangers. Her antidote is to explore the natural process of illustrating conversation and description through gesture. As she states, "**in life we 'indicate' like mad!**" (107). As an exercise, she has students use gesture to illustrate the answers to questions such as "what is a waterfall?, what is archery?, what is a helicopter?, what is pole vaulting?"(108) in order to restore a natural vocabulary of physical gesture. She then advises actors to know to whom they're talking to and what they're talking about and to place themselves clearly in that fictional geography in the acting space. This seems somewhat obvious in terms of acting technique, yet she presents it as if it were something novel: "[L]et's think together about the famous [Mark Antony] speech from *Julius Caesar* . . . Playing Antony, you have many different places to reference, all of them vital: where are Brutus and the rest? Where is Caesar's corpse lying and where are the Senate house and Lupercal? Where would you place the citizens of Rome? It is through your gestures that we, the audience, see all these things and, quite amazingly, you will feel more connected to them as your hands reach out into space towards each of them" (111). She devotes quite a bit of text to undoing the supposed years of dramatic training that instill in actors the need to not use their hands; "[Y]ou won't erase years of your hands being trained to fall limply at your sides" (113). Are drama schools really training actors to keep their hands at their sides? If so, this writer was completely unaware of it.

The next chapter deals with style, character, and comedy. Flacks defines style as "demonstrating other than naturalistic, present-day behaviors" (122). Yet she maintains that underlying feelings and emotions are universal through time. Her point of entry into period style is a character's clothing: "When you break down the elements that comprise an actor's embodiment of another period, you realize that it mostly comes down to clothing" (122). She advocates using the open "dungeon" to feel along with the character in a particular play. Actors are then advised to recognize the musicality inherent in the texts of different authors. The book's other admonitions are somewhat commonsensical—as in her advice to build a character by examining what the playwright says about him or her, what he or she says, what the given circumstances are, and what others do and say in response. Nevertheless, she continues to warn against enlisting the intellect in constructing character. In her discussion of comedy, she points out **"there's very little funnier than watching people suffer"** (128) and emphasizes the need for authentic feeling while offering sound advice on comedic rhythm.

The book's final chapter, "Auditions: Your Chance to Shine," returns to the theme of fear and repression as obstacles to success. "I remember years ago rushing to my therapist's office after an audition, feeling completely gutted. She smiled as she said, 'Ah, Niki, you only ever audition for *two people* all your life. Your mother and your father'" (135). It is imperative, she writes, to go into auditions with an open "dungeon." After recommending that the actor have several memorized audition monologues, Flacks finishes by re-emphasizing her central premise: "The real adventure is when *your opened Dungeon* speaks to the feelings locked in the Dungeons of your audience. Their Dungeon doors crack open, light filters in and you have done your work as an actor. **You have transformed your pain, your struggles, your sadness and your joy into this wondrous thing we call 'art'"** (156).

While *Acting With Passion* draws on the author's wealth of experience, and provides many useful tips on acting and auditioning, it does not offer a complete approach. Much of the criticism that she directs against Stanislavski-based training is a strawman argument framed around an outmoded stereotype of the Method. What the author paints as novel approaches in this book can be found in the authentic work of Stanislavski himself or in the physical training of Michael Chekhov. Flacks also draws on elements of Alexander Technique, and some of the exercises closely parallel aspects of Linklater voice work. I have no doubt that her approach can be effective for numerous actors who seek increased access to their emotional selves. But such an unabashedly psychotherapeutic approach is not for everyone, and the book reinforces the misapprehension that acting is primarily about feeling emotion. Authentically experiencing a character's emotions is a *necessary* but not *sufficient* element in creating a compelling performance. Emotional experience must be shaped within the context of the character, the story, and the production. Far from being a comprehensive alternative to conventional Stanislavski-based drama education, *Acting with Passion* ends up as merely one more option in the range of books dealing with generating emotions in the actor.

# NOTES ON CONTRIBUTORS

**Sally Bailey, MFA, MSW, RDT/BCT,** is a Professor of Theatre and Director of the Drama Therapy Program at Kansas State University in Manhattan, KS. Her book *Barrier-Free Theatre* was the recipient of the American Alliance for Theatre in Education's 2011 Distinguished Book Award. Previous to Kansas State, she worked for 13 years in the Washington, D.C., area as a registered drama therapist with recovering addicts and people with disabilities. A past president of the North American Drama Therapy Association, she is a recipient of their Gertrud Schattner Award for distinguished contributions to the field of drama therapy in education, publication, practice, and service.

**Rena Cook** is Professor Emeritus at the University of Oklahoma. She is also a freelance corporate voice trainer, director, actress, and voice over artist. Her book *Voice and the Young Actor* is used widely in high schools throughout the US and UK. She is a former Editor-in-chief of the *Voice and Speech Review*. Rena holds an MA in Voice Studies from the Royal Central School of Speech and Drama in London, and an MFA in directing from the University of Oklahoma. www.renacook.com.

**Cosmin Chivu** is the Director of the BA Acting and BA Directing, International Performance Ensemble at Pace School of Performing Arts. He was born in Romania and has taught and directed in America, Austria, Australia, England, Germany, Greece, Italy, Poland, Romania, and Thailand. In America, Cosmin directed plays in New York City (Lincoln Center, Cherry Lane, The Actors Studio, New Ohio, HERE Arts Center), Massachusetts (The Provincetown T. Williams Festival, KO Festival), California, and New Jersey. He is a lifetime member of the Actors Studio, a member of the Lincoln Center Directors Lab, and has completed Artist Residency programs with the Drama League, SDC, and the Jack O'Brien fellowship at the Old Globe. Since 2012, Cosmin Chivu has been the moderator of The Masters Series at Pace.

**Paige Dickinson, Ph.D., RDT/BCT,** is a Registered Drama Therapist and Board Certified Trainer, Her doctorate is in Health Psychology. She teaches in the Human Development Department at Eckerd College and is an Adjunct teaching Ethics and Drama Therapy at Kansas State University.

**Lee Evans, Ed.D.,** professor of music at NYC's Pace University, is an innovative jazz educator, author, composer, and arranger of over 100 music books in the U.S., thirty-eight in Japan, and two in the former Soviet Union, as well as the author of numerous music-magazine articles for *Clavier, The California Music Teacher, Piano Guild Notes, JAZZed,* and others. His most recent acclaimed publication is Crash Course In Chords (Hal Leonard, publisher.) A forthcoming music book of his will be titled *Classics With A Touch Of Jazz* (Edward B. Marks/Hal Leonard.) At Pace, Dr. Evans teaches Jazz History, Music Appreciation, and his enriched version of Fundamentals of Music.

**Joel G. Fink** is a Professor of Theatre in The Theatre Conservatory of Chicago College of Performing Arts at Roosevelt University and a founding director of that conservatory which he headed for thirteen years. Previous teaching: New York University, University of Colorado, Purdue University, California State University, The New School, Hunter College, and Circle-In-The-Square Theatre School. He is a Member of Actors' Equity; SAG/AFTRA; International Jugglers' Association; American Massage Therapy Association. He was casting director for Colorado Shakespeare Festival for fourteen years. In the Chicago area he directed *The Cradle Will Rock, Dear Liar,* and *The Sandbox* for the Chicago Humanities Festival; appeared in Organic/Touchstone's *Racing Demon*; worked on productions of *Cymbeline and Troilus* and *Cressida* at Chicago Shakespeare Theatre; directed *Twelfth Night* for the Illinois Shakespeare Festival and directed more than twenty productions at Roosevelt University. Additional work: Barter Theatre of Virginia, Mark Taper Forum in L.A., and Center Stage Theatre in Baltimore, among others. Dr. Fink has published numerous stage adaptations, as well as articles and reviews.

## Notes on Contributors

**Marjorie Gaines** is an Adjunct Professor of Theatre at California State University Northridge. She earned her B.F.A. in Theatre and Acting at New York University Tisch School of the Arts, and her M.F.A in Acting and Directing from California State University, Long Beach. A professional actress and member of AEA and SAG/AFTRA, Marjorie also holds a California State Single Subject English Credential with a Drama/Theatre Authorization. Marjorie has created a system of theatre courses that empower classroom teachers and non-theatre majors, as well as providing an opportunity for theater majors to make a living in the arts between – or in addition to – theater and film assignments.

**Richard Gilbert** is a Ph.D. student in the English department at Loyola University Chicago. His research focuses on representations of violence in contemporary theater, with related interests in adaptation, narrative theory, and mimetic theory. He holds an M.A. in Humanities from the University of Chicago, and a B.A. in theater from Brandeis University. He is also a professional violence designer, whose company R&D Choreography has designed over 300 productions in Chicago and around the country.

**Laurel Koerner** is an actor, director, and educator. Currently, she is the Director of Theater and Assistant Professor of Theater at Tabor College in Hillsboro, Kansas, where she teaches performance courses and directs the college's productions. Outside of academia, she works with collaborators in Los Angeles to create stage and film productions. Current endeavors include *The Radio Venceremos Project*, a play about the clandestine radio station and its role in El Salvador's civil war throughout the 1980s. Laurel received her M.A. in Theater at Bowling Green State University and her MFA in Acting at the California Institute of the Arts.

**David Krasner, Ph. D,** Dean of the School of the Arts at Dean College, has taught acting since 1978. He is the author of 11 books on acting, dramatic theory and criticism, American drama, modern drama, theatre and philosophy, and African American theatre. He twice received the Errol Hill Award from the American Society for Theatre Research and the 2008 Betty Jean Jones Award from the American Theatre and Drama Society. A student of Paul Mann, Kim Stanley, and Barbara Loden, in 2011 he performed onstage as Eddie Carbone in *A View from the Bridge* (available on YouTube).

**Jenna Lourenco, M. A.,** is a professional performer and adjunct professor of Performing Arts at Emmanuel College in Boston, MA. As a performer and director, Jenna's projects focus on historic and cultural representations such as Irish drama and the Salem Witch Trials, and on accent/dialect coaching. Jenna's academic research currently deals with the performativity of autism. She has also explored the influence of mythology on gender performativity in Irish drama. She was the 2011 recipient of the Graduate Dean's Award from Emerson College for her master's thesis on the works of Marina Carr.

**David Marcia** has a PhD in theatre from the University of Missouri, an MFA in directing from Rutgers University, and a BFA in acting from Otterbein College. He has directed regionally, off-off Broadway, and in universities. As a playwright his plays: *Lust of the Flesh and the Wiles of Sin*, *Coward Land*, and *What Breaks Your Heart?* were semi-finalists at the Eugene O'Neill National Playwrights Conference.

**Kathleen Mulligan** is an Associate Professor of Voice and Speech at Ithaca College. In 2010 she was a Fulbright-Nehru Scholar to Kerala, India, with her project "Finding Women's Voices," focusing on the empowerment of women through voice. She spent the spring of 2015 in Pakistan as a Fulbright specialist collaborating on her project "Voices of Partition" with husband David Studwell and members of Islamabad's Theatre Wallay. The resulting piece *Dagh Dagh Ujala (This Stained Dawn)*, based on interviews with survivors of the Partition of 1947, toured to Ithaca, Boston, and Washington, D.C., in October 2015. The project was funded by a grant from the U.S. Embassy in Islamabad and the Fulbright organization. She is a proud member of Actors' Equity Association. Acting credits include The Acting

Company (national tour), American Repertory Theater, Fort Worth Shakespeare in the Park, and PCPA Theatrefest in Santa Maria, CA.

**Kevin Otos** is an Associate Professor of Theatre at Elon University where he teaches a variety of contemporary and classical acting courses, movement, and also directs. Professional directing credits include three seasons at the Texas Shakespeare Festival and the North American premier of Simon Stephens' *Pornography* at the Burning Coal Theatre. Also a professional actor, some favorite roles include Antony in *Julius Caesar* and Antonio in *The Merchant of Venice*. He can also be seen on the television series *One Tree Hill* and *Necessary Roughness*. Kevin recently directed and adapted *The Servant of Two Masters*, and is regularly asked to conduct workshops on the Commedia dell'Arte and other areas of expertise at conferences and universities. You can learn more about Kevin at www.kevinotos.com.

**Mark Rafael** is a professional actor, educator, and communication consultant. A graduate of Brown University and the Yale School of Drama, he is currently a professor at the University of San Francisco. He also teaches at the American Conservatory Theater and the Academy of Art University. He is the author of *Telling Stories: A Grand Unifying Theory of Acting Techniques*. He has appeared in many Bay Area Theaters as well as Yale Repertory, American Stage, Wisdo Bridge, and Northlight Theatre, among others. His film and television credits include *Titanic, Trauma, Star Trek Voyager, The Practice*, and *Babylon 5*.

**Dennis Schebetta** is assistant professor and head of the M.F.A. Performance Pedagogy program at the University of Pittsburgh. Professionally, he has worked as an actor, playwright, dramaturg, and director in film and theatre, both regional and Off-Off Broadway at the Ensemble Studio Theatre, Vital Theatre, Pittsburgh Playhouse, Bricolage, City Theatre, 13th Street Rep, 12 Peers, and the HERE Arts Center. He trained as an actor in the two-year Meisner program with William Esper at his studio in New York and most recently studied with master Shakespeare teacher John Basil. He has taught

Shakespeare as a teaching artist for the Pittsburgh Public Theatre and has taught at Carnegie Mellon University, Bellevue College, and Virginia Commonwealth University, where he earned his MFA in Theatre Pedagogy.

**Tom Smith** is a playwright, director, and associate professor of Theatre at Pacific Lutheran University. His plays are published by Samuel French, Playscripts, and YouthPLAYS, among others and have been produced in Australia, Belgium, Canada, Germany, Ireland, Latvia, Netherlands, New Zealand, Romania, Sweden, Switzerland, and the United Kingdom. Tom is also the author of *The Other Blocking: Teaching and Performing Improvisation* (Kendall Hunt) and articles and reviews for *Theatre Journal, Theatre Topics*, and several resource books. He is a proud member of the Dramatist's Guild and Stage Directors and Choreographers Society.

**Bara Swain** has an M.F.A. from the New School for Social Research. She has served as an editor/reviewer at *Flash Fiction Magazine, Bellevue Literary Review, Fantastic Flash Fiction Anthology* (Pandemonium Press), *Care Management Journals*, and *Daifuku* chapbooks. Her plays have been performed in more than 100 venues in 19 states, and are anthologized by publishers Smith & Kraus, Art Age Press, Applause Books, Original Works Publishing, Meriwether, and JAC Publications. "Critical Care" serves as a key reading for the craft of playwriting in *Serious Daring*, Oxford U. Press. Currently, Bara is the Creative Consultant at Urban Stages.

**Leigh Woods** has taught at the University of Michigan since 1987 and has served as Head of Theatre Studies during that time. He's written extensively about performance and the history of acting in *Garrick Claims the Stage, On Playing Shakespeare, Public Selves/Political Stages* (with Agusta Gunnarsdottir), and *Transatlantic Stage Stars in Vaudeville and Variety*. He has co-edited *Playing to the Camera*, and his articles have appeared in *Theatre Survey, Theatre Journal, Scandinavian Review, Shakespeare Quarterly, Shakespeare Yearbook, Essays in Theatre, Theatre Research International, New*

*Theatre Quarterly, The Arthur Miller Journal,* and *Contemporary Theatre Review*. A member of the Actors' Equity Association, he's performed over 100 roles onstage, including American premieres of plays by George W. D. Trow, Heiner Müller, and Wendy Wasserstein, and most recently played Leonato in *Much Ado About Nothing*.

**Robert Woods** is well-versed in the business of acting as an entertainment lawyer in Los Angeles. He has negotiated contracts between producers and actors, both stars and neophytes. He has represented clients on both sides in lawsuits: producers against actors, actors against producers, and even talent agencies and managers in dispute with the actors they represent. As a producer, Woods has worked with casting directors and has cast both stars and regular working actors in three films made for television, including an award-winning TV movie. Woods has also cast and directed actors in stage productions from Los Angeles to New York to China, and was an actor himself in more than thirty plays and musicals. In addition to his law degree, Woods also holds an M.F.A. in Directing. He taught acting classes at the University of Oklahoma School of Drama, and is currently teaching a business law course at The Los Angeles Film School. All of this experience has convinced Woods that it is essential for young actors to be taught business skills, not only to help them succeed, but to keep them from making costly mistakes as they pursue their careers.

**Rebecca Worley** is an Assistant Professor of Theatre at Texas A&M University, Commerce, and a PhD candidate at Southern Illinois University. She is a dramaturg, educator, and director. Her primary areas of interest are political theater, protest as performance, feminist theory, and theatre pedagogy. Her work explores the ways theatre is a tool for social transformation. She has presented papers at ATHE, MATC, and TETA. Currently, Ms. Worley serves as the Coordinator for TETA's Academic Symposium. Most recently, she presented her paper, "The Triangle Factory Fire Project: the Work of an Embodied Archive in Performance," at ATHE.

## Call for Essays, Book Reviews, and Editors

*Methods* is a peer-reviewed journal on actor training published annually by Pace University Press. The journal aims to promote and disseminate research on all matters related to the training of actors: new exercises, innovative techniques and philosophies, discussion of principal texts and methodologies; any subject related to acting will be considered. Submissions and inquiries will be acknowledged immediately. Articles will be anonymously peer-reviewed. The MLA Style format is required. There are no length requirements or limitations.

We also seek book reviewers and editors for initial readings and recommendations. For book reviews contact Dr. Charles Grimes at grimesc@uncw.edu and to act as part of the editorial board contact Dr. Ruis Woertendyke at rwoertendyke@pace.edu. Also email Dr. Woertendyke for more information, proposals, abstracts, and submissions.

**Abstracts for Volume 3 Due**     12/15/16
**Articles Due**     4/10/17

## Colophon

This second volume of *Methods: A Journal of Acting Pedagogy*
was published in Fall 2016
by Pace University Press

Cover and Interior Design by Sara Yager assisted by Rachel Diebel
The journal was typeset in Minion Pro and Myriad Pro
and printed by Lighting Source in La Vergne, Tennessee

**Pace University Press**
Director: Sherman Raskin
Associate Director: Manuela Soares
Marketing Manager: Patricia Hinds
Graduate Assistants: Rachel Diebel and Taylor Lear
Student Aide: Kelsey O'Brien-Enders

CPSIA information can be obtained
at www.ICGtesting.com
Printed in the USA
FSOW02n0043030817
37077FS